Copyright Policies
and Workflows
in Libraries

Copyright Policies and Workflows in Libraries

A Concise Handbook

ALLYSON MOWER

ROWMAN & LITTLEFIELD
Lanham • Boulder • New York • London

Published by Rowman & Littlefield
An imprint of The Rowman & Littlefield Publishing Group, Inc.
4501 Forbes Boulevard, Suite 200, Lanham, Maryland 20706
www.rowman.com

6 Tinworth Street, London SE11 5AL, United Kingdom

British Library Cataloguing in Publication Information Available

Library of Congress Cataloging-in-Publication Data Available

ISBN 9781538133217 (cloth: alk. paper) | ISBN 9781538133224 (pbk. : alk. paper) | ISBN 9781538133231 (electronic)

∞™ The paper used in this publication meets the minimum requirements of American National Standard for Information Sciences—Permanence of Paper for Printed Library Materials, ANSI/NISO Z39.48-1992.

Contents

Preface

Copyright, as a system of rights and exceptions, helps define authorship, ownership, and reuse of content. This system becomes relevant to librarians in their mission of creating a demand for knowledge, supporting the generation of new ideas, and connecting people to information and content. Librarians also provide services surrounding the creation of new content, making the copyright system important on an additional level.

Simply put, copyright consists of six rights (copy, adapt, distribute, display, perform, transmit) and ten exceptions, including an entire exemption dedicated to libraries and archives open to the public. Becoming familiar with the core rights is the easy part! Knowing them will help you quickly determine when the copyright system gets engaged within your library. Navigating the exceptions as they relate to librarians and libraries is the trickier part. When incorporated into a policy, exceptions can provide consistent guidance on when and how much librarians and information professionals can engage in the exclusive rights both with or without permission.

Copyright Policies and Workflows in Libraries will cover several topics. We will start with copyright eligibility and duration then work our way through rights and exceptions, move to a discussion about partnering with attorneys to develop a policy relevant to your library and/or institution, and end with ways of implementing and incorporating the policy into daily practice and determining its effectiveness. As we go through these various topics (or if you ever

feel like you are stuck in the copyright weeds), keep in mind the broader purpose of copyright to promote the arts and sciences. Developing products of the
mind takes time and effort on the part of authors, artists, and other creators.
Remember that what they create is warranted some protection so that they can
retain some control over their intellectual property. But also keep in mind that
some control is the operative phrase. There are many exceptions to ensure that
not just rights holders can determine the progress of arts and sciences.

Librarians certainly have a role in ensuring that progress as part of our professional duties. We also have a role in supporting the system that provides
writers, artists, scientists, and their publishers with the economic sustenance
needed to continue creating. Yes, the rules can seem impossible, arcane, and
utterly ignorable, but I believe that librarians and information professionals
have it in them to become fully informed experts and great defenders of accuracy in our provision of copyright information and library services.

One of the main ends of librarianship is to create a demand for knowledge,
and incentivizing the creation of new knowledge is what underpins the copyright system. This creates a synergistic connection, in my opinion, between
librarianship and the copyright system. To protect the expressions inherent
in new ideas is why copyright exists. As librarians, we place new and relevant
works in the hands of readers, learners, inventors, creators, and writers.
Knowing what is relevant to the communities we serve is a significant challenge that many of us address in a myriad of ways ranging from book displays
and readers' advisory to speaker programs and makerspaces. Many times, the
most relevant works needed to create that demand for knowledge are going
to be the newest works, and that means they will also be copyrighted works.
Older works where the copyright has expired can also greatly contribute to
the creation of new knowledge. Understanding the copyright rules regarding
new and older works can be challenging, but I would argue that they are less
challenging than trying to determine what is relevant to a local community.
It takes time (and a little patience) to become familiar with the copyright
system, just as it takes time (and arguably even more patience) to know the
hearts and minds of the population librarians support.

One of the reasons librarians and information professionals can become
frustrated with copyright stems from the general amount of misinformation
about copyright. Some of it is perpetuated by our own profession, but it can
also come from publishers and other content providers. This misinforma-

tion is especially pernicious in the realm of digitized content. Be mindful of publishers and content providers who claim copyright in works they have digitized. Many times, there is a misunderstanding among digitizers that the process of scanning a work automatically creates a new copyright. But, as you will learn in this book, that is not the case. There is a term in the copyright lexicon called "copyfraud," simply defined as erroneously claiming rights to a work of authorship. Chapter 1, "Copyright Basics," will help librarians and information professionals learn how to detect copyfraud.

Besides misinformation causing frustration amongst our profession regarding copyright, the range of opinions about the general purpose of copyright can also contribute. Some people are copyright maximalists and others are copyright minimalists. This means some think the arts and sciences will progress more rapidly the longer a copyright lasts (the maximalists) and others think advancement will come at a quicker pace the shorter a copyright lasts (the minimalists). Same goes for the fair use exception. Some think it is merely a defense against infringement, and others think that it is a right instead of an exception. It is useful for these debates to happen both within and outside our profession, but it is also important for librarians and information professionals to not let the cultural commentary and copyright advocacy get in the way of providing accurate information about copyright and well-informed library services.

The American Library Association's Code of Ethics guides our profession in the provision of library services. The first principle focuses on providing accurate and unbiased responses to patron requests, which is important to keep in mind, but the fourth principle is the most salient for this book because it discusses copyright by affirming that librarians, as a profession, "respect intellectual property rights and advocate balance between the interests of information users and rights holders."[1] Copyright policies can assist in furthering both the first and fourth ethical principle. Taken together, these two principles remind us as librarians that we strive for high-level accuracy as well as a balanced approach to advocating for both copyright holders and information users. In this regard, this means we remain as objective as possible when answering copyright questions. Policies and procedural workflows support such objective information practices.

It is difficult to say how many copyright policies exist in libraries throughout the United States. A 1984 ARL SPEC Kit provides copies of copyright policies from thirty-four research libraries.[2] In a 2005 study of copyright reuse policies and practices in research libraries, information scientists found that "many institutions have adopted copyright policies of some form," but did not provide an exact count.[3] In another study from 2013, researchers found that thirty research libraries had a copyright policy in place to govern course reserve services.[4]

The journal literature on library copyright policies emphasizes academic libraries over other types of libraries including public, government, school, private, and special. One international study attempted to survey digital collection managers from all types of libraries (national, public, academic), but only received responses from managers in academic libraries.[5] Obviously, librarians in all kinds of libraries engage with copyright. A basic web search for the phrase "library copyright policies" returns results from hundreds of public, school, government, and private libraries. This book includes eight of these policies as examples in chapter 5, "Sample Policies."

So, what is a policy? In general, policies serve as simple communication mechanisms. Ideally, they relay a common and shared understanding regarding definition of terms, permissible activities, and behaviors in the context of the relevant local entity that has developed and promulgated the document. They represent a form of governance especially for complex organizations that serve or involve people such as governments, schools, and large workplaces. Even on a smaller scale, policies can represent what a small business owner expects of her employees or even what a teacher expects of students in a classroom. In most instances, policies are written and drafted by a group of people representing the broader entity or organization.

In addition to serving as communication mechanisms, policies also regulate behavior and serve as a tool of governance. One of the first social policies in human history, according to political scientist Mark Schrad, dates to "the initial discovery of the inebriating effects of alcohol on the human body and mind." Schrad argues that "attempts to regulate the consumption of alcohol have existed for hundreds, if not thousands, of years—thus establishing alcohol control historically as the first social policy."[6] Policies often have a bad reputation because they can be out-of-touch, not reflective of broader practices, stifling instead of empowering, and mundane. All of these can be true to some extent.

With some good design practices, policies can go beyond the mundane to the higher plane of problem-solving. Think of policies (and your role within them) as being systematically creative. One way to achieve good policy making is to have a firm understanding of good policy design. With the end goal in mind, think of the policy as the guidance an individual who is part of the organization would need in order to achieve that goal. For example, if a library director's goal is to ensure that librarians do not engage in copyright infringement, then the library director would seek to draft a copyright policy that would detail for employees what would count as infringement and what would not. Many voices, including those who have working knowledge of the copyright statute, would need to be reflected in the policy document. But it would be the library director who recognized the problem or need and communicated the end goal of the policy.

Goals and the policies to support them do not always have to come only from managers or administrators. It is possible for a non-manager librarian to have a goal in mind for the library where she works. The process would be the same. The librarian would articulate the goal to those around her as well as to those who serve as managers and supervisors, get consensus on the goal, and then build consensus to proceed with policy drafting. For example, say the librarian overseeing scanners, copiers, and printers wanted to communicate a user's responsibility when it comes to the copying of copyrighted works. That type of policy would look slightly different than the policy clarifying what library employees can copy. The difference would stem from the distinction in goals as well as audience.

Good policies consist of a clear mission, achievable goals, and consistent communication. In light of good governance, policies become a type of support system rather than a hindrance or mere arbitrary set of rules and regulations. Policies can also be bolstered by best practices or even a distinct set of workflows, depending on the nature of the policy. In terms of copyright policies, having specific workflows associated with the document can be incredibly empowering for an individual librarian, especially one who might not be familiar with the details of copyright.

A set of steps for people to follow in order to achieve the end goals of the policy can be incorporated into the policy document itself or they can stand outside the document and receive a reference in the policy. The best option will depend on the goal of the policy. If the purpose of the policy is to ensure that library employees do not infringe someone's copyright or mistakenly claim ownership to a digitized work, then it would make sense to include the necessary procedures into the policy document in order to avoid such outcomes. If the goal of the policy is to communicate to library users what is expected of them, step-by-step instructions probably would not be necessary.

Workflows help achieve the requisite clear communication embedded in effective governance. They prepare those impacted with the necessary tools to successfully adhere to a policy. Without them, there is a risk that a policy can seem meaningless. If the rules of your draft policy feel complex and layered, then consider adding detailed instructions as its own section of the document.

Workflows, as standalone documents, are very common in libraries, especially in technical service areas. One of the more common examples is having both a collection development policy and a set of procedures to go along with it. Creating both a copyright policy as well as a workflow would follow this same example. Standalone copyright workflows are not as common as other types of workflows, but some libraries do have them. The HathiTrust Digital Library has one of the most robust copyright research workflows, which they have posted on their website: https://www.hathitrust.org/rights_database.

Rachel Bridgewater writes about a copyright permission workflow used in the reserve department at the Washington State University Vancouver library.[7] The Revs Institute also has a documented copyright workflow for a mass digitization project that commenced in 2012.[8] On a historical note, researchers have uncovered that ancient Assyrians used bilateral documents to not only control the distribution of goods and commodities, but to also dictate to workers the type of work expected regarding the commodities. The writing on clay tablets has been interpreted to show a listing of commodities and supplies along with the proposed "activities of employees."[9] A copyright policy plus a workflow could perhaps be considered a kind of modern-day bilateral document.

While copyright can sometimes feel like trying to understand an ancient clay tablet, the contents of this book hope to make it feel less foreign. This guide attempts to bring together copyright and librarianship by detailing the ways in which elements of both can be incorporated into policies and workflows. The book offers information about policy making, collaboration, and implementation. The goal of this volume is to assist librarians and information professionals in designing policies and procedures that will offer the assistance, clarity, accuracy, and consistency about copyright that fellow librarians and information professionals in your institution and library users in your community may have sought.

Librarians and information professionals encounter copyright situations on a daily basis, from interlibrary loan and electronic reserves to book displays, digital archiving, and publishing. Most books on copyright focus on helping librarians understand basics—the best ones include *The Librarian's Copyright Companion, 2nd Edition* by James Heller, et al. and *Getting Permission: How to License & Clear Copyrighted Material Online & Off* by Richard Stim—but none of them detail how to create copyright policies and workflows relevant to the work of librarians. I have found that having a policy along with a research workflow means you do not have to read the copyright statute every time someone has a copyright question. Instead, a copyright policy provides quick and easy access to copyright information so that you can efficiently provide a library service or answer a patron's copyright question.

I have served as a copyright librarian for ten years, crafted an institutional fair use policy, created several copyright research workflows, and trained other librarians both inside and outside my own organization on implementing policies and workflows. I wanted to write this book because having a copyright policy helps librarians and information professionals know how and when they have engaged in the exclusive rights and the ways in which the many exceptions of copyright can be applicable to our work, when we should seek permission, and when to encourage our patrons to do so.

Many librarians and information professionals have talked to me about their frustrations with copyright. And many of my colleagues throughout the region have sometimes reacted to copyright situations in extremes. I have heard many librarians say that we should always say no when it comes to patrons requesting to copy something; I have heard others say that all copying and public distribution done by librarians and information professionals is fair use. Neither of these beliefs are fully accurate. With this book, perhaps there will be enough information to make copyright situations less extreme and a little more balanced and practical. I suggest adding several books to your copyright information arsenal in order to ground yourself more firmly in good information about copyright. See Resources and Further Reading for more information.

Part of the frustration with copyright could stem from the fact that copyright is a federal law and laws are complex and scary. It can be frightening for librarians and information professionals to think of themselves as inadvertently providing legal advice. I struggle with this every day. There is a fine line between providing information about a law and providing legal advice, but there is a line. I encounter this fine line on a daily basis in my provision of copyright information services, and it has been the driver behind creating policies and workflows. The policy—created in partnership with attorneys—established a buffer between me in my professional role as librarian and the law. This means I simply provide information about what the institution's copyright policy says. I quote from it and point patrons to it by including links and specific references. It also means I do not have to quote from or link to the statute, which helps protect me from being perceived as providing legal advice. When I do have to mention something directly from the statute, I clarify that I am delivering information only and not providing any advice about what a person should or should not do in their copyright situation.

All of this is to say that *Copyright Policies and Workflows in Libraries* does not provide legal advice. It encourages librarians and information professionals to familiarize themselves with the copyright system in order to provide good information about copyright in the provision of services and to serve as full partners in drafting a policy in collaboration with relevant and applicable attorneys.

NOTES

1. American Library Association. "ALA Code of Ethics, Article IV." Last modified January 22, 2008. http://www.ala.org/tools/ethics.

2. Kranich, Nancy. *Copyright Policies in ARL Libraries.* Washington, DC: Association of Research Libraries, 1984.

3. Gould, Thomas H. P.; Lipinski, Tomas A.; Buchanan, Elizabeth A. "Copyright Policies and the Deciphering of Fair Use in the Creation of Reserves at University Libraries." *Journal of Academic Librarianship* 31, no. 3 (2005): 182–197.

4. Hansen, David R.; Cross, William M.; Edwards, Phillip M. "Copyright Policy and Practice in Electronic Reserves among ARL Libraries." *College & Research Libraries* 74, no. 1 (2013): 69–84.

5. Koulouris, Alexandros; Kapidakis, Sarantos. "Policy Route Map for Academic Libraries' Digital Content." *Journal of Librarianship and Information Science* 44, no. 3 (2012): 163–173.

6. Schrad, Mark Lawrence. "The First Social Policy: Alcohol Control and Modernity in Policy Studies." *Journal of Policy History* 19, no. 4 (2007): 428–451.

7. Bridgewater, Rachel. "Shifting Responsibility for Electronic Reserves Copyright Permissions from the Academic Departments to the Library: From Confusion to Cooperation." *Journal of Interlibrary Loan, Document Delivery & Electronic Reserve* 18, no. 2 (2008): 141–152.

8. Vargas, Mark A.; Bright, Jessica. "Rev Your Engines: Racing Ahead with Mass Digitization." *Computers in Libraries* 37, no. 7 (2017): 4–8.

9. Postgate, Nicholas. *Bronze Age Bureaucracy: Writing and the Practice of Government in Assyria.* Cambridge, UK: Cambridge University Press, 2014.

Acknowledgments

To Alyssa for all the dedication and all the intelligent debates, to my parents David and Diane, and to the following entities that graciously allowed their copyright policies to be included in the book:

Auburn Public Library in Auburn, Maine

Ecological Society of America in Washington, DC

King County Law Library in Seattle, Washington

Louisville Catholic Schools in Louisville, Kentucky

National Park Service Office of Policy in Washington, DC

Snow College Libraries in Ephraim, Utah

Somerset County Library System in Somerville, New Jersey

University of Utah in Salt Lake City, Utah

1

Copyright Basics

In this chapter, we will cover copyright eligibility, core rights, and duration. Fair use gets defined in context of librarianship and policy development. Reproduction by Libraries & Archives also gets defined for purposes of establishing a library copyright policy. Additional exemptions to the core rights listed within the Copyright Act that are relevant to some libraries are included along with how permissions and licensing operate in relation to copyright policies.

This chapter provides details on how to recognize the pieces of copyright in order to build a good policy and improve library services. The information is organized to highlight the most salient aspects of copyright for the profession. It is ordered in a way that will prepare readers for drafting or revising a copyright policy.

Overall, the chapter addresses long-standing confusion in the library, archives, museum, and cultural heritage fields regarding the practice of claiming copyright ownership to works that have been digitized. Addressing the confusion will provide clarity and will make it easier for librarians and information professionals to understand what they can and cannot claim copyright ownership to. Knowing the basics and having even a cursory knowledge of the exemptions—especially fair use and reproduction by libraries and archives—will help librarians and information professionals improve their practice and make policy drafting more straightforward and consistent with the Copyright Act.

COPYRIGHT ELIGIBILITY

For librarians and information professionals, it is important to have a solid understanding of copyrightability. We work with a range of content that can come from any number of authors, time periods, and publishers/content providers. We lease and purchase content, house material within our buildings, and preserve it. We own material and we create material. Within such an ecosystem, it can be hard to distinguish between physical property ownership and intellectual property ownership and to ferret out accurately who owns what when it comes to copyright-related library services. A good place to start is to constantly keep in mind copyright eligibility. Knowing this fundamental piece of copyright can even mean skipping a reference to a policy because if a work is not eligible for copyright protection, then the rules for reuse are open.

The phrase I continually use to help me distinguish between intellectual ownership and physical ownership is *product of the mind*. To be eligible to receive protection, a work needs to be a product of the mind. Examples include literary, dramatic, musical, and artistic works. Secondly, the product of the mind needs to be original to the author and slightly creative. The other eligibility requirement includes fixation, meaning the product of the mind has to be fixed in a tangible medium in order for there to be a copyright. It is probably rarer for librarians and information professionals to come across a work not fixed, so let us focus more on the importance of originality.

One helpful way to understand copyrightability is to become familiar with examples of ineligible works listed in the *Compendium of U.S. Copyright Office Practices, Third Edition.*[1]

Works Ineligible for Copyright Protection

1. Reducing or enlarging the size of a preexisting work of authorship.
2. Making changes to a preexisting work of authorship that are dictated by manufacturing or materials requirements.
3. Converting a work from analog to digital format, such as transferring a motion picture from VHS to DVD.
4. Declicking or reducing the noise in a preexisting sound recording or converting a sound recording from monaural to stereo sound.
5. Transposing a song from B major to C major.
6. Medical imaging produced by X-rays, ultrasounds, magnetic resonance imaging, or other diagnostic equipment.

7. A claim based on a mechanical weaving process that randomly produces irregular shapes in the fabric without any discernible pattern.

For librarians and information professionals, examples #1 through #3 are the most relevant to become familiar with and will help in both the day-to-day provision of library services as well as crafting copyright policies.

Physical Property Ownership Is Not Intellectual Property Ownership

Converting a work from analog to digital is something we as librarians engage in daily. When you think about it, this process of converting a work from one format to another does not involve an original output of the mind. While perhaps requiring technical expertise, digitization is merely a mechanical process. Its output contains no originality or unique expression, two hallmarks of copyright eligibility. The *Compendium* says that "copyright law only protects 'the fruits of intellectual labor' that are 'founded in the creative powers of the mind.'"[2] It also indicates that "copyright law is limited to 'original intellectual conceptions of the author.'" In other words, if the work you are looking at was made by someone who simply scanned it, then the person who made the scan is not the copyright holder because the person did not independently create the work as a product of her intellect. Separating the concepts of physical and intellectual property ownership can help your library move forward in developing clearer copyright policies.

Physical property ownership means that a library holds an item in its collection. The item can either be purchased or donated. Physical ownership means librarians and information professionals who work at the library get to decide how to take care of an item, including where it gets placed in the library, the level of description it requires, any labeling placed on the material, and rules regarding its access and circulation. As the physical property owner, librarians and information professionals can even decide, and communicate to others, the way in which the library prefers to be attributed and noted as the entity that holds the item.

Many responsibilities come with owning and holding an item in a library, but owning the intellectual rights embodied in a work are not included. By simply possessing a work, a library does not become a rights holder. For a library to become a rights holder, the original copyright holder would need to transfer or assign those rights to the library by written agreement. If that written transfer has not been made, then those rights stay with the person (or corporate entity) who created the work. Neither owning an item nor converting it to another format establishes a copyright for a library. It is, in fact, quite rare for a library to be a rights holder. It is possible, but rare. Libraries primarily act as physical property owners and not intellectual property owners.

Even without a written assignment, the library that holds an item is not completely at the whim of the rights holder when it comes to making decisions about caretaking, access, and description. There are exceptions spelled out in the statute that make it possible for librarians and information professionals to operate and run their libraries without being bogged down by having to get permission from rights holders. Libraries primarily rely on Section 109 the First Sale doctrine when it comes to lending and circulation. The other main exceptions include Section 107 Fair Use and Section 108 Libraries & Archives. Fair Use and Libraries & Archives will get covered in more detail later in this chapter, especially as they relate to copyright policies.

Products of the Mind

What are the creative powers of the mind? Let us look to the fields of psychology and cognitive science to get a better sense of what that means. Cognitive scientists Gilles Fauconnier and Mark Turner have indicated that "modern human imagination [has provided] the ability to invent new concepts and to assemble new and dynamic mental patterns" and that this form of imagination emerged in humans approximately 50,000 years ago during the Upper Paleolithic Age.[3] Concepts that Fauconnier and Turner say came forth during this time included language, art, science, religion, tools, and culture. Their research shows that this type of mental capacity developed because of a cognitive operation called conceptual blending. It is a process that happens in the background to produce visible manifestations and cognitive products. They describe conceptual blending as playing "a decisive role in human thought and action" as the mind creates conceptual packets, schematic frames, and long-term memory.

Concepts such as language, says arts educator Ken Robinson, play a role in producing thoughts. Once thoughts are developed, imagination and imaginary thinking can form, and from imagination comes creative powers of the mind, Robinson argues. Creativity also requires action and needs to involve media beyond the mind so that the thought or idea can be manifested or expressed. Robinson calls creativity a "dialogue between the ideas and the media in which they are being formed."[4] He lists various media such as wood, plastic, stone, and paper in which to express ideas and imagination. As you may recall from the previous section on eligibility, copyright protects the expression of ideas fixed in a tangible medium.

CORE RIGHTS AND DURATION

When a work is eligible for protection, certain rights get extended to authors for a limited time. This bullet list shows a shortened version of each right in order to highlight the activity associated with each right. By focusing on the active verb, it becomes easier, in my experience, to quickly know when my colleagues or I are engaged in any of the exclusive rights. Those rights include the following:

- To reproduce the work
- To prepare derivative works
- To distribute copies of the work
- To perform the work publicly
- To display the work publicly
- To transmit sound recordings

I like to keep track of them by counting on my fingers each operative activity: copy, distribute, display, adapt, perform, transmit. This shorthand helps me know when I should consult the policy.

Elements of the core rights have distinct meanings that would need to be incorporated into a definitions section of a policy. Defining the terms will assist everyone who has to adhere to the policy. Since copyright comes from a statute, the definitions used in the policy should match what is in the statute. Ensuring that they match represents why it is important for librarians to partner with their institution's attorneys in crafting the document.

The descriptions of each core right used below come from the glossary of the *Compendium* rather than the statute as a way of ensuring that readers of this book do not inadvertently rely on it as legal advice and instead use the book as a guide to inform themselves in preparation to discuss further with a relevant attorney. Here is how the U.S. Copyright Office explains the role of the *Compendium*:

The *Compendium* does not override any existing statute or regulation. The policies and practices set forth in the *Compendium* do not in themselves have the force and effect of law and are not binding upon the Register of Copyrights or U.S. Copyright Office staff. However, the *Compendium* does explain the legal rationale and determinations of the U.S. Copyright Office, where applicable, including circumstances where there is no controlling judicial authority.

The *Compendium* more fully defines the exclusive rights:

Exclusive rights: Any or all of the exclusive rights under Copyright Law, as set forth in Section 106 of the Copyright Act. Section 106 of the Copyright Act defines the exclusive rights of copyright owners in their works. Only the copyright owner has the right to do and to authorize the following:

1. "To **reproduce** the copyrighted work in copies or phonorecords."
2. "To **prepare derivative works** based upon the copyrighted work."
3. "To **distribute** copies or phonorecords of the copyrighted work to the public by sale or other transfer of ownership, or by rental, lease, or lending."
4. "In the case of literary, musical, dramatic, and choreographic works, pantomimes, and motion pictures and other audiovisual works, to **perform** the copyrighted work publicly."
5. "In the case of literary, musical, dramatic, and choreographic works, pantomimes, and pictorial, graphic, or sculptural works, including the individual images of a motion picture or other audiovisual work, to **display** the copyrighted work publicly."
6. "In the case of sound recordings, to perform the copyrighted work publicly by means of a digital audio **transmission**."

17 U.S.C. § 106. These rights are subject to certain limitations that are defined in Sections 107 through 122 of the Copyright Act.

The bolded words represent terms that get defined further in the *Compendium* and may also represent terms that would need to get defined in a draft copyright policy. Whether or not they get defined in a policy will depend on the type of policy that is needed. To determine the type of policy needed will depend on the goal of the librarian or information professional implementing the policy as discussed earlier.

Relevant Copyright Terms from the *Compendium* Glossary[5]

Audiovisual work: "'Audiovisual works' are works that consist of a series of related images which are intrinsically intended to be shown by the use of machines or devices such as projectors, viewers, or electronic equipment, together with accompanying sounds, if any, regardless of the nature of the material objects, such as films or tapes, in which the works are embodied." 17 U.S.C. § 101. In other words, the term "audiovisual works" refers broadly to any work that includes any series of related visual images, whether or not moving, and with or without sounds, as long as a machine or device is essential to the viewing of the related series of images.

Copies: "'Copies' are material objects, other than phonorecords, in which a work is fixed by any method now known or later developed, and from which the work can be perceived, reproduced, or otherwise communicated, either directly or with the aid of a machine or device. The term 'copies' includes the material object, other than a phonorecord, in which the work is first fixed." 17 U.S.C. § 101.

Derivative work: "A 'derivative work' is a work based upon one or more pre-existing works, such as a translation, musical arrangement, dramatization, fictionalization, motion picture version, sound recording, art reproduction, abridgment, condensation, or any other form in which a work may be recast, transformed, or adapted. A work consisting of editorial revisions, annotations, elaborations, or other modifications, which, as a whole, represent an original work of authorship, is a 'derivative work.'" 17 U.S.C. § 101.

Display: "To 'display' a work means to show a copy of it, either directly or by means of a film, slide, television image, or any other device or process or, in the case of a motion picture or other audiovisual work, to show individual images nonsequentially." 17 U.S.C. § 101.

Literary works: "'Literary works' are works, other than audiovisual works, expressed in words, numbers, or other verbal or numerical symbols or indicia, regardless of the nature of the material objects, such as books, periodicals, manuscripts, phonorecords, film, tapes, disks, or cards, in which they are embodied." 17 U.S.C. § 101. A literary work is a nondramatic work that explains, describes, or narrates a particular subject, theme, or idea through the use of narrative, descriptive, or explanatory text, rather than dialog or dramatic action. Generally, nondramatic literary works are intended to be read; they are not intended to be performed before an audience. Examples of nondramatic literary works include the following types of works: fiction, nonfiction, poetry, directories, catalogs, textbooks, reference works, advertising copy, compilations of information, computer programs, databases, and other textual works.

Perform: "To 'perform' a work means to recite, render, play, dance, or act it, either directly or by means of any device or process or, in the case of a motion picture or other audiovisual work, to show its images in any sequence or to make the sounds accompanying it audible." 17 U.S.C. § 101.

Phonorecords: "'Phonorecords' are material objects in which sounds, other than those accompanying a motion picture or other audiovisual work, are fixed by any method now known or later developed, and from which the sounds can be perceived, reproduced, or otherwise communicated, either directly or with the aid of a machine or device. The term 'phonorecords' includes the material object in which the sounds are first fixed." 17 U.S.C. § 101.

Publication: "'Publication' is the distribution of copies or phonorecords of a work to the public by sale or other transfer of ownership, or by rental, lease, or lending. The offering to distribute copies or phonorecords to a group of persons for purposes of further distribution, public performance, or public display, constitutes publication. A public performance or display of a work does not of itself constitute publication." 17 U.S.C. § 101.

Public performance and public display: "To perform or display a work 'publicly' means

1. to perform or display it at a place open to the public or at any place where a substantial number of persons outside of a normal circle of a family and its social acquaintances is gathered; or
2. to transmit or otherwise communicate a performance or display of the work to a place specified by clause (1) or to the public, by means of any device or process, whether the members of the public capable of receiving the performance or display receive it in the same place or in separate places and at the same time or at different times." 17 U.S.C. § 101.

Defining "Reproduce"

You will notice that "reproduce" as a verb has no definition in the *Compendium* glossary. There is no definition in the statute, either. Circular 21, published by the U.S. Copyright Office, uses the phrases "the making of copies" and "the making of phonorecords" and defines that activity as "photocopying, making microform reproductions, videotaping, or any other method of duplicating visually-perceptible material and [. . .] by duplicating sound recordings, taping off the air, or any other method of recapturing sounds."[6] Since many librarians and information professionals reproduce works in various situations and contexts, it would be useful for purposes of a library copyright policy to take the time to define "reproduce" as it relates to the goal of the policy. The definition may be as basic as "to make a copy" or "to produce again" or a basic listing of example activities similar to what Circular 21 indicates: photocopying, scanning, digitizing, downloading, microfilming. Having this type of list in a policy would provide library professionals with more concrete details.

DURATION

For works created after 1978, copyright protection lasts for the life of the author plus seventy years. For works created before 1978, different duration amounts, terms, and requirements exist. The Public Domain Slider, part of the American Library Association's (ALA) Copyright Toolkit at http://www .ala.org/advocacy/copyright-tools, comes in very handy when needing to determine various requirements and a copyright term.

The *Compendium* also goes into greater detail on duration of copyright based on changes to the Copyright Act in 1909 and 1992. It is rare, but it could be possible, to include a definition of duration in a library copyright policy. This would make sense if the policy intended to guide library employees on both copyright ownership and copyright expiration. Like the definition of "reproduce," it could be as simple as stating that the exclusive rights last for a certain period of time and that library employees are encouraged to utilize tools such as the Public Domain Slider to determine duration.

Duration could also get relabeled as "public domain" and then afforded a fuller definition. This would be particularly useful for libraries that serve schools, colleges, and universities and those that maintain digital or special collections. Such a definition would assist policy readers in knowing, more

FIGURE 1.1
Public Domain Slider available from ALA's Copyright Toolkit. *Toolkit http://www.ala .org/advocacy/copyright-tools.*

precisely, what constitutes a copyrighted work. Remember, once a copyright has expired, it becomes an uncopyrighted work and the work is no longer eligible for protection, not even if it gets digitized. Defining duration or public domain would again bring to the surface the basic requirements of originality and fixation discussed above. It could serve as a reminder and a reinforcement of these fundamental facts. Having such definitions in place could also go a long way in addressing the prevalence of many digital collections to claim ownership of and require permission for digitized versions of works that happened to have been held on physical shelves.

To review, a copyrighted work is one which has met the legal definition of authors having fixed an expression of an idea in a tangible medium using a modicum of originality in the process. A copyrighted work would be one which is still within the time frame of protection allotted by the statute. Newer works of authorship, such as those created sometime in the last three decades, would be considered copyrighted works. Older works of authorship, those published in the 1800s and early 1900s, would be non-copyrighted works. Other non-copyrighted works would include works not of human authorship, those without originality, and those not fixed in a tangible medium.

Now that we have a solid understanding of the fundamentals of copyright such as authorship, eligibility, core rights, and duration, let's move on to some of the exceptions to the core rights that get spelled out in the statute. With at least ten exceptions, understanding them all can feel overwhelming and unmanageable. By focusing on the ones relevant to librarians and information professionals as well as those based on library types (e.g., school and academic), they can start to seem more practical and even handy as a quick guide to what seekers can and cannot do within the copyright system.

The exceptions below get listed in numerical order as they appear in the statute. You might recall the numbering referenced in the *Compendium* above. The *Compendium* first mentions Section 106. This section covers the core rights. As a continuation from Section 106, the next section is 107, and begins the listing and discussion of the various limitations on the exclusive rights.

DEFINING FAIR USE (SECTION 107)

This exception to the core rights helps ensure that information seekers can reproduce works of authorship for the purpose of critiquing, teaching, or researching without needing the permission of the rights holder. It helps ensure free speech, free expression, and intellectual freedom. For librarians who work with teachers, scholars, journalists, and/or freelance writers, it is important to maintain familiarity with fair use in order to provide accurate information to patrons.

Many librarians I have worked with over the years have thought that all work of libraries, including marketing and public relations, is covered by fair use, but as seen in the list below, that is not the case. Fair use is powerful, but it is limited to certain purposes. To establish a definition of fair use for a policy, consider combining the list of purposes and factors as described below.

List of Fair Use Purposes
- Criticism
- Comment
- News Reporting
- Teaching
- Scholarship
- Research

Fair Use Factors
- Purpose and character of the use
- Nature of the work to be used
- Amount of the work to be used
- Effect of the use on the market for the work

Including a definition of fair use becomes most relevant for school and academic librarians because they primarily serve teachers, learners, researchers, and scholars. But the list does not end there. Libraries that serve journalists, artists, musicians, or writers would also want to include a solid, working definition of fair use as a way to guide the librarians and information professionals who help patrons doing this type of work. Placing the definition into the policy will take out the guesswork for library employees who will inevitably be faced with questions about how much of a copyrighted work in the library's collection can be copied. Before even hazarding a guess, the librarian—knowing the fuller definition of fair use via the library's policy—would initially want to clarify that there is an exception that allows for copying when critiquing, teaching, or studying a work. There would be a quick reference interview in that the librarian could ask about the patron's purpose and then proceed to explain what the library's policy says regarding amount.

The purposes and factors come directly from the Copyright Act. You will hear some people say that fair use is a doctrine or principle, and you will hear others say that any and all uses are fair. But, of course, the truth is somewhere in the middle. Fair use is codified, making it more than a doctrine, but it is also limited to certain purposes. By becoming familiar with the purposes, it will make the balancing of the factors easier to do when working with a patron.

These factors work in tandem, and you would evaluate the use by considering the balance of the four. For a documented evaluation, point your patrons to the Fair Use Evaluator available in ALA's Copyright Toolkit. If your library provides services for teachers, researchers, independent scholars, writers, artists, or fellow librarians and that service includes copying or any of the other core rights, then you also need to be familiar with the four factors that go in to considering whether any copying or distributing is fair so that you can accurately guide your patrons in their work.

If your library engages in its own criticism or comment on a work of authorship by publishing a blog, newsletter, or podcast, then you would con-

FIGURE 1.2
Fair Use Evaluator from ALA's Copyright Toolkit. *Toolkit http://www.ala.org/advocacy/ copyright-tools.*

sider the four factors for your library's own use. You would also rely heavily on your library's copyright policy. Chapter 4 provides more details on how a policy and evaluation go hand in hand. The important takeaway from this section is becoming familiar with the list of purposes allowed within the fair use exception.

Unfortunately, the *Compendium* glossary does not include a definition of fair use that could be easily incorporated into a draft policy. This is because the U.S. Copyright Office does not directly deal with the range of exceptions (other than to mention their existence in the definition of Exclusive Rights). On the bright side, there are examples of libraries with copyright policies that have defined fair use in various ways that can serve as a guide. Some refer to the educational fair use guidelines initially developed in the 1980s that discuss the threefold test of brevity, spontaneity, and non-cumulative use.[7] Others combine fair use with other exceptions such as Libraries & Archives as this one does:

> Under certain conditions specified in the "fair use" provision of copyright law, libraries and archives are authorized to furnish users a photocopy or reproduction. The photocopy or reproduction may be used "for purposes such as

criticism, comment, news reporting, teaching (including multiple copies for classroom use), scholarship or research," but not for commercial purposes.[8]

A couple of policies use definitions that pretty closely mirror the statute, but this one goes far beyond it by listing a reference to the exclusive rights, which I have bolded for easy reference:

Fair use allows people and organizations to **reproduce, modify, distribute, display, and publicly perform** works created by others in certain circumstances and for certain purposes, including criticism, comment, news reporting, teaching, scholarship, or research. In addition to the purpose and character of the proposed use, fair use requires consideration of the nature of the copyrighted work, the amount and substantiality of the portion of the original work used, and the effect of the use upon the potential market for (or value of) the copyrighted work.[9]

This one keeps the definition very close to what the statute says:

Fair use—is a reasonable noninfringing use, including reproduction, of copyrighted material for such Purposes as criticism, comment, news reporting, teaching, scholarship or research, as determined from consideration of all relevant circumstances, including (1) the Purpose or character of the use, e.g., for commercial Purposes or for nonprofit educational Purposes, (2) the nature of the copyrighted work, (3) the amount and substantiality of the portion used in relation to the copyrighted work as a whole, and (4) the effect of the use upon the potential market for or value of the copyrighted work.[10]

Here is the exact wording from Section 107 of Title 17 of the United States Code:

107. Limitations on exclusive rights: Fair use
Notwithstanding the provisions of sections 106 and 106A, the fair use of a copyrighted work, including such use by reproduction in copies or phonorecords or by any other means specified by that section, for purposes such as criticism, comment, news reporting, teaching (including multiple copies for classroom use), scholarship, or research, is not an infringement of copyright. In determining whether the use made of a work in any particular case is a fair use the factors to be considered shall include—

(1) the purpose and character of the use, including whether such use is of a commercial nature or is for nonprofit educational purposes;

(2) the nature of the copyrighted work;

(3) the amount and substantiality of the portion used in relation to the copyrighted work as a whole; and

(4) the effect of the use upon the potential market for or value of the copyrighted work. The fact that a work is unpublished shall not itself bar a finding of fair use if such finding is made upon consideration of all the above factors.

Fair use represents one of many exceptions to the exclusive rights. While it remains broad in scope, it is not unlimited. For librarians and information professionals to meet the profession's code of ethics in balancing the rights of copyright owners with the greater goal of creating a demand for knowledge, knowing the exact scope of the exception is crucial. Providing accurate information ensures not only that we follow our professional standards, but that we also maintain trust within our communities. Figuring out what is accurate about copyright in a world where diffuse and unreliable information about the topic has built up and spread over time can be challenging. The challenge can be addressed by including carefully crafted definitions within a copyright policy. Helga Nowotny has said in her book *The Cunning of Uncertainty* that policies represent "institutionalized forms of coping with uncertainty."[11] The copyright system can definitely be one of those uncertainties. Not only does a copyright policy need to include a definition of fair use so that librarians can provide accurate information to patrons, it also needs to define the scope of the Libraries & Archives exemption to guide ourselves in the provision of our work in libraries and archives.

REPRODUCTION BY LIBRARIES & ARCHIVES (SECTION 108)

This exception to the core rights ensures that librarians and archivists can preserve and maintain access to works of authorship. Get prepared to see a much longer list of allowable activities than we saw in the fair use exception. The longer list is both a blessing and a curse—greater flexibility for collections, but more for librarians to keep track of! Like the fair use exemption, the Libraries & Archives exemption does not cover a library's marketing, promotion, or public relations activities.

The easiest way to become familiar with Section 108 is to know that is has nine subsections. Most of them are directly related to traditional library services such as interlibrary loan, preservation, and copy machines in the library so it is easy to work through them:

Subsections of the Libraries & Archives Exemption
a) Qualifying for the Exemption
b) Copying Unpublished Works
c) Copying Published Works
d) Articles or Excerpts for Users
e) Out-of-Print Works
f) Copiers & Scanners plus Fair Use
g) Provisos
h) Preservation & Term Extension
i) Music, Pictures, Graphs, Sculptures

The details of each subsection get covered later in the book, but the important aspect to know at this point is that you can incorporate this exception into your library's copying policy. ALA's Copyright Toolkit also provides a quick guide to the exception with the Section 108 Spinner.

FIGURE 1.3
Section 108 Spinner from ALA's Copyright Toolkit. *Toolkit http://www.ala.org/advocacy/ copyright-tools.*

Since the U.S. Copyright Office deals primarily with matters of registration, eligibility, and authorship and not as much on the various exceptions, the *Compendium* does not include extensive discussion about Section 108. The U.S. Copyright Office, however, publishes Circular 21, as mentioned above, to provide more information on Section 108. They also have a web page dedicated to Section 108 in support of the study group it convened with the National Digital Information Infrastructure in 2006 to look at digital technology as it relates to the work done in libraries and archives.[12]

To be eligible for the Libraries & Archives exemption, the library and its collections have to be open to the public and not-for-profit. Public libraries that have a copyright policy will sometimes limit it to Section 108 and not include fair use within the document. This can be a useful way to provide for the specific goal of adhering to the exemption, but it can also mean missing out on the chance for librarians to work with patrons who are not library employees and any of their fair use-related purposes as well. Most libraries with copyright policies, though, rarely mention Section 108 and instead focus on Section 107. I imagine that if any private libraries had copyright policies they would also only include Section 107. Since there is a special exception related to public libraries, I would argue for combining both Section 107 and Section 108 into a single policy document.

The nine subsections contain all the relevant details that would get incorporated into a policy. Here's how Section 108 and the subsections get described in the Copyright Act:

108. Limitations on exclusive rights: Reproduction by libraries and archives

(a) Except as otherwise provided in this title and notwithstanding the provisions of section 106, it is not an infringement of copyright for a library or archives, or any of its employees acting within the scope of their employment, to reproduce no more than one copy or phonorecord of a work, except as provided in subsections (b) and (c), or to distribute such copy or phonorecord, under the conditions specified by this section, if—

  (1) the reproduction or distribution is made without any purpose of direct or indirect commercial advantage;
  (2) the collections of the library or archives are (i) open to the public, or (ii) available not only to researchers affiliated with the library or archives or with

the institution of which it is a part, but also to other persons doing research in a specialized field; and

(3) the reproduction or distribution of the work includes a notice of copyright that appears on the copy or phonorecord that is reproduced under the provisions of this section, or includes a legend stating that the work may be protected by copyright if no such notice can be found on the copy or phonorecord that is reproduced under the provisions of this section.

(b) The rights of reproduction and distribution under this section apply to three copies or phonorecords of an unpublished work duplicated solely for purposes of preservation and security or for deposit for research use in another library or archives of the type described by clause (2) of subsection (a), if—

(1) the copy or phonorecord reproduced is currently in the collections of the library or archives; and

(2) any such copy or phonorecord that is reproduced in digital format is not otherwise distributed in that format and is not made available to the public in that format outside the premises of the library or archives.

(c) The right of reproduction under this section applies to three copies or phonorecords of a published work duplicated solely for the purpose of replacement of a copy or phonorecord that is damaged, deteriorating, lost, or stolen, or if the existing format in which the work is stored has become obsolete, if—

(1) the library or archives has, after a reasonable effort, determined that an unused replacement cannot be obtained at a fair price; and

(2) any such copy or phonorecord that is reproduced in digital format is not made available to the public in that format outside the premises of the library or archives in lawful possession of such copy.

For purposes of this subsection, a format shall be considered obsolete if the machine or device necessary to render perceptible a work stored in that format is no longer manufactured or is no longer reasonably available in the commercial marketplace.

(d) The rights of reproduction and distribution under this section apply to a copy, made from the collection of a library or archives where the user makes his or her request or from that of another library or archives, of no more than one article or other contribution to a copyrighted collection or periodical issue, or to a copy or phonorecord of a small part of any other copyrighted work, if—

(1) the copy or phonorecord becomes the property of the user, and the library or archives has had no notice that the copy or phonorecord would be used for any purpose other than private study, scholarship, or research; and

(2) the library or archives displays prominently, at the place where orders are accepted, and includes on its order form, a warning of copyright in accordance with requirements that the Register of Copyrights shall prescribe by regulation.

(e) The rights of reproduction and distribution under this section apply to the entire work, or to a substantial part of it, made from the collection of a library or archives where the user makes his or her request or from that of another library or archives, if the library or archives has first determined, on the basis of a reasonable investigation, that a copy or phonorecord of the copyrighted work cannot be obtained at a fair price, if—

(1) the copy or phonorecord becomes the property of the user, and the library or archives has had no notice that the copy or phonorecord would be used for any purpose other than private study, scholarship, or research; and

(2) the library or archives displays prominently, at the place where orders are accepted, and includes on its order form, a warning of copyright in accordance with requirements that the Register of Copyrights shall prescribe by regulation.

(f) Nothing in this section—

(1) shall be construed to impose liability for copyright infringement upon a library or archives or its employees for the unsupervised use of reproducing equipment located on its premises: Provided, That such equipment displays a notice that the making of a copy may be subject to the copyright law;

(2) excuses a person who uses such reproducing equipment or who requests a copy or phonorecord under subsection (d) from liability for copyright infringement for any such act, or for any later use of such copy or phonorecord, if it exceeds fair use as provided by section 107;

(3) shall be construed to limit the reproduction and distribution by lending of a limited number of copies and excerpts by a library or archives of an audiovisual news program, subject to clauses (1), (2), and (3) of subsection (a); or

(4) in any way affects the right of fair use as provided by <u>section 107</u>, or any contractual obligations assumed at any time by the library or archives when it obtained a copy or phonorecord of a work in its collections.

(g) The rights of reproduction and distribution under this section extend to the isolated and unrelated reproduction or distribution of a single copy or phonorecord of the same material on separate occasions, but do not extend to cases where the library or archives, or its employee—

(1) is aware or has substantial reason to believe that it is engaging in the related or concerted reproduction or distribution of multiple copies or phonorecords of the same material, whether made on one occasion or over a period of time, and whether intended for aggregate use by one or more individuals or for separate use by the individual members of a group; or

(2) engages in the systematic reproduction or distribution of single or multiple copies or phonorecords of material described in subsection (d): Provided, That nothing in this clause prevents a library or archives from participating in interlibrary arrangements that do not have, as their purpose or effect, that the library or archives receiving such copies or phonorecords for distribution does so in such aggregate quantities as to substitute for a subscription to or purchase of such work.

(h)(1) For purposes of this section, during the last 20 years of any term of copyright of a published work, a library or archives, including a nonprofit educational institution that functions as such, may reproduce, distribute, display, or perform in facsimile or digital form a copy or phonorecord of such work, or portions thereof, for purposes of preservation, scholarship, or research, if such library or archives has first determined, on the basis of a reasonable investigation, that none of the conditions set forth in subparagraphs (A), (B), and (C) of paragraph (2) apply.

(2) No reproduction, distribution, display, or performance is authorized under this subsection if—

(A) the work is subject to normal commercial exploitation;

(B) a copy or phonorecord of the work can be obtained at a reasonable price; or

(C) the copyright owner or its agent provides notice pursuant to regulations promulgated by the Register of Copyrights that either of the conditions set forth in subparagraphs (A) and (B) applies.

(3) The exemption provided in this subsection does not apply to any subsequent uses by users other than such library or archives.

(i) The rights of reproduction and distribution under this section do not apply to a musical work, a pictorial, graphic or sculptural work, or a motion picture or other audiovisual work other than an audiovisual work dealing with news, except that no such limitation shall apply with respect to rights granted by subsections (b), (c), and (h), or with respect to pictorial or graphic works published as illustrations, diagrams, or similar adjuncts to works of which copies are reproduced or distributed in accordance with subsections (d) and (e).

Don't be overwhelmed by the bulk of the text. Just remember there are nine subsections and work your way through one at a time. It will become easy to manage once you become familiar with the various subsections.

ADDITIONAL EXEMPTIONS TO THE CORE RIGHTS RELEVANT TO LIBRARIES

The fair use and Libraries & Archives exemptions deal primarily with copying, which make them the most relevant when developing a library policy on the copying of copyrighted works. There are other exemptions relevant to the work of librarians and information professionals, however, that are good to generally be aware of. First Sale doctrine (Section 109) allows for lending copies of works of authorship and to publicly display them. Face-to-Face Teaching (Section 110) is an additional exception to the exclusive right of displaying a work publicly. And Section 117 (Computer Programs) makes an exception for creating a personal backup of computer software.

Be aware of these exceptions as you start to work with your institution's attorneys so that you can decide together, depending on the type of library where you work, whether these additional exceptions should be incorporated.

GETTING PERMISSION

When none of the exceptions apply, then permission to copy, distribute, display, adapt, perform, or transmit gets obtained from the rights holder. There are many ways to get permission. You can check for the work at the Copyright Clearance Center. You can do a general web search using the rights holder's name to find contact information. Most publishers will have dedicated copyright permission web pages with email addresses and request forms. Many times, the registration record available through the online catalog of the U.S. Copyright Office will have contact information. I have even successfully used Twitter to locate and connect with an artist for permission to use a book cover for library event advertising. Another good resource is WATCH: Writers, Artists, and Their Copyright Holders.

Sometimes fees come with a permission. Other than royalty rates set for music by the U.S. Copyright Royalty Board, there is no set amount. It depends on the rights holder, the type of work, and the broader industry that the content is a part of. It is always possible to negotiate a permission fee, however, and many times rights holders provide permission without charging a fee.

It could make sense to add a definition of permissions to a library copyright policy. There are no examples to point to, but having a definition would certainly help librarians and information seekers know how the permissions process works within the copyright system. A simple definition of "permissions" in the context of copyright would look something like this:

Permissions—sought out when a use of a third-party copyrighted work does not fall within the exceptions described in this policy. Forms of permission include licensing through a publisher, Copyright Clearance Center, directly with a rights holder, or by means of an existing, web-based license such as Creative Commons.

Copyright
United States Copyright Office

Help Search History Titles

Public Catalog

Copyright Catalog (1978 to present)

Basic Search   Other Search Options

Search for:

Search by:
Scroll down for
Search Hints

Title (omit initial article A, An, The, El, La, Das etc.)
Name (Crichton Michael; Walt Disney Company)
Keyword
Registration Number (for VAu 598-675 type vau000598675)
Document Number (for V2606 P87 type v2606p087)
Command Keyword

25 records per page

Begin Search   Reset

FIGURE 1.4
Catalog of Registration Records. *https://cocatalog.loc.gov/*.

LICENSING

Although no documents I have come across have done this, you could take the library's policy one step further and also define licensing as a type of permission as a way to capture the fuller range of options. Here's a sample definition:

> Licensing—a type of permission where terms regarding the reuse of copyrighted works get presented upfront. Any reuse terms agreed to are documented separately from this policy.

Depending on the nature of the work and the licensing scheme, some terms go through a negotiated agreement process whereby both parties stipulate what can and cannot be done with the copyrighted work or works. The transparency of licensing terms will come in varying degrees ranging from a license that can be read by everyone, such as a Creative Commons or Terms of Use posted on a website, to terms only accessible to those internal to an organization. Typically, terms that are less transparent are that way because of practical purposes such as getting stored in either paper or electronic format within an internal-only records management system. Others are intentionally not accessible because the parties agree to not disclose details to outside entities.

Obviously, this level of detail would get unwieldy in a policy document, but a basic mention of potential licensing practices within the context of a broader entity such as a city or county government, school district or academic institution could be useful information for both library employees and end users.

Point Policy Readers to Resources

As we discussed earlier, every policy will have an end goal. If it turns out that the goal of the policy that you help draft includes ensuring that librarians and information professionals in your institution can successfully refer information seekers to quality resources, then consider adding a section on related resources. In that section, policy drafters could include guides to finding licensed resources, getting permission, conducting fair use evaluations, determining expiration dates, or internal copyright research workflows.

Chapter 4 will cover copyright workflows, but our next chapter will cover how to outline and write a policy based on these copyright basics. We will also delve in to how to make a policy official.

NOTES

1. U.S. Copyright Office. *Compendium of U.S. Copyright Office Practices, Third Edition.* Washington, DC: U.S. Copyright Office, 2017, 17.

2. Ibid., 4.

3. Fauconnier, Gilles; Turner, Mark. *The Way We Think: Conceptual Blending and the Mind's Hidden Complexities.* New York: Perseus Books Group, 2002.

4. Robinson, Ken, Sir. *Out of Our Minds: The Power of Being Creative.* Chichester, West Sussex, UK: John Wiley & Sons, 2017.

5. U.S. Copyright Office. *Compendium of U.S. Copyright Office Practices, Glossary.* Washington, DC: U.S. Copyright Office, 2017.

6. U.S. Copyright Office. *Reproduction of Copyrighted Works by Educators and Librarians, Circular 21.* August 2014. Accessed March 15, 2019. https://www.copyright.gov/circs/circ21.pdf.

7. Ibid.

8. California State Library. *Copyright Policy.* Accessed April 5, 2019. http://www.library.ca.gov/california-history/fair-use/.

9. University of California. *Copyright.* Accessed April 5, 2019. http://copyright.universityofcalifornia.edu/resources/copyright-fair-use.html.

10. University of Utah. *Policy 7-013: Copyright Policy: Copying of Copyrighted Works.* Accessed April 5, 2019. https://regulations.utah.edu/research/7-013.php.

11. Nowotny, Helga. *The Cunning of Uncertainty.* Malden, MA: Polity Press, 2016.

12. U.S. Copyright Office. *Section 108.* Accessed March 25, 2019. http://www.section108.gov/index.html.

2

Writing a Policy and Making It Official

In this chapter, we will cover how to draft, revise, and obtain approval for a copyright policy. We will discuss ways of placing your library in context and how to become familiar with governance and collaboration within individual libraries and institutions. The chapter includes a drafting worksheet as well as a sample approval workflow to give readers a sense of how to get policies and procedures approved. With a clear goal in mind and a solid grasp of the approval process, policy drafters will know who to work with in their institution and what to include in the document.

The main difficulty in writing a policy and making it official can arise from not fully understanding the purpose of the policy and not knowing the approval process at an individual institution. To make the work more manageable, policy writers will need to create a plan. As we discussed earlier, library directors, managers, and policy drafters will need to ask themselves what the policy will help librarians and information professions within a library or institution achieve. Librarians in a non-administrative position can also ask themselves if work would become easier and clearer with a copyright policy in place. The outcome needs to become clear in the minds of the policy drafters and implementers first before work can proceed. Who the policy would impact within the library or institution, especially regarding whose work it would change, also needs to be thought out and fully considered.

This chapter will give readers the opportunity to think through all of these components and provide guidance on possible ways to start and proceed. Return to this chapter for relevant details as snags happen along the way. Just like the information-seeking process that librarians and information professionals help patrons with on a daily basis, policy writing and approval is iterative. Progress can be slow and even feel sluggish at times, but don't give up! As long as the initial goal and purpose are solid, the writing and approval will ultimately be successful no matter the inherent snags, roadblocks, or hurdles.

SEARCH FOR EXISTING COPYRIGHT POLICIES

The best way to begin establishing a copyright policy is to determine whether there is a current policy to work from. Start by looking through any workplace policy and procedure manuals. These policies can sometimes get buried or mislabeled. The copyright policies at the academic institution where I work are categorized as research policies. Government agencies sometimes list them within acceptable use and employee behavior policies. It is also possible for them to get categorized as computer and security policies or simply as a Digital Millennium Copyright Act takedown policy. Sometimes copyright policies get labeled or titled generally as intellectual property policies, so look for those types of documents as well.

Depending on the type of library where you work, you might find two copyright policies: one dealing with the reuse of copyrighted content and another detailing work-for-hire and copyright ownership. For purposes of this book, you will want to focus only on finding the policy related to reuse (although if you are a copyright librarian, you will certainly want to also look at any ownership policies). If you work for a public library, look for any policies from the relevant government agency, such as city, county, state, or tribal government.

Ask your co-workers if they are aware of any copyright policies. Not only will having conversations help you locate any documents, they will also help seed future conversations about developing one, in the event that one is not in place or an existing one needs major revising. Talk to both long-term employees, new ones, and those in management positions.

If there is an existing policy (or several of them), the next step is to spend time reading it in order to familiarize yourself with what types of policies— whether reuse, copyright ownership, acceptable use, security/computer—

currently govern your library, agency, or institution, and then plan next steps. If no policy exists, then consider drafting one. It can feel daunting, but, hopefully, with this book and with the support of colleagues, the work can be manageable.

An easy way to determine what type of policy you are reading is to look at both the title and the definitions of terms. Some policies will have the vague title of "copyright policy," but the introductory terms and definitions will quickly let you know if the policy is about ownership or reuse.

For example, the Mt. Pleasant School Library in Rolla, North Dakota, titles their policy "Copyright Policy," but the very first line of the policy indicates that the document pertains to Section 107 of the Copyright Act. This signals that the policy is a reuse policy because it focuses on the fair use exemption.

In another example, the Oxford Public Library in Oxford, Michigan, labels their policy "Copyright Infrigement [sic] Policy." This could mean that it is a reuse or acceptable use policy, but upon closer reading, the policy details the notice and takedown procedures the library will utilize if a rights holder finds any infringing material at the library's web address. It does not speak to any goals or expectations of librarians or information professionals who are employed by the city of Oxford, nor does it address patron reuse except to the extent of defining any actions the library will take regarding what they label "repeat infringers."

Chicago Public Library in Chicago, Illinois, uses a similar approach by naming its policy "Copyright and Takedown Policy." It addresses takedown procedures, but also includes a very brief section on reuse for both patrons and library employees.

Auburn Public Library in Auburn, Maine, simply calls their policy "Copyright," but the very first line indicates that its goal is to ensure compliance with the Copyright Act. This makes it a reuse policy, and they elected to include both patrons and library employees in a single policy. West Chester Public Library in West Chester, Pennsylvania, places their policy within the library's policy manual and titles it "Copyright Compliance" and directs it to employees only. Salt Lake City Public Library in Salt Lake City, Utah, also places their policy within the library's policy manual, but it does not use the word "copyright" as a label. Instead, it places copyright details in the website section of the policy manual, which falls under the broader category of "communication."

Reuse terms as well as ownership get included in California State Library's policy, which they title "Copyright Policy." The EcoEd Digital Library, a nonprofit library provided by the Ecological Society of America, also covers ownership as well as reuse in their policy labeled as "Copyright and Terms of Use." Neither the California State Library nor EcoEd use their policies to communicate goals or govern employee behavior when it comes to the copying of copyrighted works.

Louisville Catholic Schools in Louisville, Kentucky, places their copyright policy within a document called "Library Media Guidelines." The guidelines get produced and promulgated by the Archdiocese of Louisville. Based on the goals enumerated in the introduction, the policy is a reuse policy. It mentions all of the copyright exemptions (Sections 107 through 121), but focuses primarily on Section 107 Fair Use. The policy does not distinguish between employee types—teachers or librarians—when it comes to reuse, but it does seem to be written more for teachers than for librarians since none of the sections incorporate Section 108 Libraries & Archives.

In contrast, King County Law Library in the state of Washington has exclusively a Section 108 policy with the stated goal of conformance on the part of library employees. The policy is referred to as a copyright policy and includes a short section for patrons, but is primarily geared toward library services and library employees. The policy does not incorporate fair use or work-for-hire copyright ownership.

Both fair use and ownership get included in the Sauquoit Valley Central School Copyright Policy. The policy resides within a manual for the school district located in Sauquoit, New York, and applies to employees (both teachers and librarians), board members as well as students. It also includes elements of the Face-to-Face Teaching exemption (Section 110[1]) under a brief section categorized for audiovisual material.

The University of California system does not include a reference to any teaching exemptions in their policy called "Copyright and fair use." It is a reuse policy (ownership is separate) that pertains to all employees and students in pursuit of the university's teaching, research, and public service goals. The policy also indicates a commitment on the part of the university's counsel to defend employees as part of an infringement claim, making this both a reuse as well as an infringement policy.

As you can see, copyright policies get named and categorized in various ways. This simply means that it might take more time than anticipated to find the policy or policies governing your library.

PLACING YOUR LIBRARY IN CONTEXT

As you work to determine if a current copyright policy exists, you will begin to realize where your library fits in the broader context. School and academic libraries fit within a school district, college, or university. Some can be private, some can be public. Public libraries fit within a city, county, tribal area, or state. Private and special libraries fit within a larger company. Sometimes libraries stand on their own. The point is to think about the nature of your library and where it fits. Because copyright is a legality, knowing your library's context will greatly inform how to seek out, outline, organize, write, redraft, and get a policy approved.

To begin contextualizing your library, think about three key aspects of library operations: funding source, decision-making and governance, and patron base or clientele. Knowing funding sources and decision-making surrounding funding will assist policy drafters in both the writing and approval process. It is also important to be cognizant of the general role of the library where you work. Look at your library's mission, vision, and value statement. Think about the type of people the library serves and whether the library's patrons or clientele play roles in pursuit of their information seeking. The role of a researcher might be a different role than a teacher. Copyright will apply differently to both of those kinds of workers. As we discussed previously, there are at least two copyright exemptions for teachers, but not as many for researchers. Your library's context will also help you know what type of approvals and reviews will be needed to get a legally based policy in place.

Possible funding sources could include property taxes, memberships, internal allocations, grants, or a combination of these sources. In terms of governance, consider who mainly determines either the source or the allocation of the library's budget: library director, administrators outside the library, library board, or a combination of these roles and groups. Then think about whom your library considers as its main clientele: local residents, employees, students, patients, or a combination of these populations.

For example, if property taxes fund your library, a library board helps determine allocation along with the library director, and your main clientele are local residents, then you would be considered a public library, be it city, municipality, county/parish, tribal, or state. If your library's budget comes as an allocation from another budget that gets determined by administrators outside the library and your library primarily serves students and employees such as teachers or researchers, then you would be considered a school, academic, or research library.

Obviously, any librarian who ends up spearheading policy drafting will know what type of library he or she works for. This information is not solely to help drafters figure out their library type, but instead, the purpose of this section is to assist policy drafters in knowing how to determine the individual people involved in library budgeting and decision-making so that a copyright policy can be fully drafted, approved, and implemented. Collaboration will be key to getting the policy written, approved, and in place.

FINDING THE RIGHT COLLABORATORS

In addition to knowing a little more about budget source and decision-making in the library, it will also help to know how general, non-budget decisions get made in the library. Librarians and information professionals use all kinds of governance strategies: internal committees or teams, no committees, library director plus library board, people outside the library, or a combination of these roles and groups. Maybe your library or institution has a committee solely dedicated to policies and procedures. Or perhaps the library director makes decisions only in consultation with a small committee or board. Or maybe your library has a committee just for copyright matters. It could be that your library has a combination of all three approaches. This will make drafting and approval somewhat difficult and time-consuming, but knowing the governance infrastructure upfront will eliminate much of the potential headache.

It could be that the library where you work has a flat structure without committees or even ill-defined governance. Keep in mind that nearly all libraries will have a manager, director, dean, or executive officer. If you are a librarian or information professional in a non-management position and at a library with no clearly defined governance structure, initiate a conversation with the main library administrator. Express your interest in the library having a policy to help guide employees and patrons on copyright matters. If you have any recent examples of confusion surrounding copyright or even an example of not being able to fully assist a library patron or information seeker because of uncertainty on how to proceed, mention them as reasons to revise or draft a new policy. Present the library director with a potential policy outline, a plan for how to reach out to the relevant attorneys, and a list of fellow library employees to potentially work with.

If you are a library director within a flat organization, consider forming a temporary task force to determine if a copyright policy is needed or requires updating. Look for librarians and information professionals who are directly engaged in copyright-related work: teaching librarians, document delivery and interlibrary loan employees, digital library workers, preservation librarians, or archivists. Have a potential goal in mind based on your own understanding of copyright, librarianship, professional ethics, and your library's context. Then brainstorm with the task force on expanding or refining the goal in a way that will make the work of librarians and information professionals easier and more straightforward within the library's operations.

Use similar strategies as a non-manager librarian. As you begin the conversation with the library's administrator, include potential colleagues in your drafting, approval, and implementation plan. Look for colleagues who might have to deal with copyright in their daily work: children's librarians, public relations officers, digital collection managers, or those overseeing copiers, scanners, or printers in the library. As you approach your fellow librarians and information professionals, keep the conversation about clarity and efficiency instead of about copyright infringement or violations. This will make the policy drafting less fearful and put everyone in a state of mind that is more forward-looking and positive rather than punitive.

REVISING EXISTING POLICY

With an existing document in hand, read through it on your own to determine what might need fixing. As you are reading, think about the general concepts that would go into a strong and useful policy: goal and purpose, definitions, copyright exemptions, and specific rules for the appropriate audience (e.g., library employees vs. patrons or library users). Make a note or comment in the document about what is missing, poorly defined, or misplaced.

Next, find the attorneys for your city, county, company, school, or institution. Review the draft with them and have a conversation about the possibility of incorporating any missing pieces such as purpose or exemptions like Libraries & Archives and First Sale. The drafting worksheet provided later in the chapter can serve as an outline to guide the conversation with the attorneys. If definitions are missing from the existing policy, try to schedule more than one meeting with the attorneys in order to have enough time to create and add new ones. Possible terms to define include the following (chapter 1 includes definitions from the *Compendium*):

- Audiovisual works
- Copies
- Derivative work
- Display
- Exclusive rights
- Fair use
- Literary works
- Perform
- Phonorecords
- Publication
- Reproducing/Reproduction
- Use
- Work

DRAFTING A NEW COPYRIGHT POLICY
If no policy exists, then a policy writer will need to start from scratch. Consider this basic outline for writing a copyright reuse policy:

1. Purpose
2. Mission or scope of the library
3. Definitions
4. Policy
   - General rules for library employees
   - General rules for library users
   - Permissions
5. Policy Owner

The drafting worksheet later in this chapter provides space to fill in details and test ideas. Details of what to place in the policy will be informed by this book as well as conversations with peers and colleagues. A policy drafter will want to first initiate conversation among library employees regarding the purpose of the policy and the statement of the library's role and mission. When embarking on those initial conversations, make the discussion about whether the existing mission statement of the library is sufficient for the copyright policy. The answer to that question will be informed by the overall goal and purpose of the policy.

Purpose

Policy goals will be centered initially on behavior of librarians and information professionals. If desired by the institution the library serves, the policy could have an additional goal of guiding the behavior of library users as well. The short list of possible policy-based goals includes the following:

- Adhering to ALA Code of Ethics
- Reducing confusion about the copying and distribution of copyrighted works
- Reducing confusion about the performance and display of copyrighted works
- Clarifying copyright eligibility of digitized works
- Defining ownership of copyrightable works created by library employees
- Guiding library patrons and users on their rights and responsibilities

Mission

The statement regarding the library's mission or scope can be informed by the library's existing mission statement as well as any conversation with fellow librarians and information professionals if the mission or scope needs to be tailored to the context of a copyright or fair use policy. Possible scoping statements could include the following:

- Library A ensures access to knowledge for all residents and provides instructional programming. As such, library employees adhere to the Libraries & Archives exemption, the First Sale doctrine, and the Face-to-Face Teaching exemption in achieving the mission.
- Library B creates a demand for knowledge among students and teachers. As such, library employees develop original, copyrightable works and tailored

collections. This policy governs rules of ownership and the exemptions of Fair Use, Libraries & Archives, and First Sale, which guide librarians, teachers, and students.

- Library C serves the information needs of health care workers and lab researchers. As such, library employees adhere to Fair Use and Libraries & Archives exemptions in achieving the mission.

Definitions

Use the policy to define key copyright terms. Not only will this help make the policy easier to understand, the definitions will also establish common copyright terminology for the library, institution, or broader community. In turn, the policy will assist in reducing confusion among library employees. The extent of the copyright overview section will depend on the context of the library, the type of patrons that librarians and information professionals serve, and the range of services that library employees offer. Possible terms to define include the following (chapter 1 includes definitions from the *Compendium*):

- Audiovisual works
- Copies
- Derivative work
- Display
- Exclusive rights
- Fair use
- Literary works
- Perform
- Phonorecords
- Publication
- Reproducing/Reproduction
- Use
- Work

Policy—General Rules

Which general rules to include will depend on the purpose, mission, and scope sections. At this point in the policy document, drafters would work carefully with relevant attorneys on ensuring that the appropriate terms from the statute are included and utilized accurately. Possible sections could include these:

- Copying for access
- Copying for preservation
- Copying for lending
- Copying for commentary
- Copying and transmitting for teaching
- Copying and transmitting for research
- Displaying copyrighted works
- Performing copyrighted works
- Responsibilities for notices and warnings
- Obtaining permission

Policy Owner and Contact

The owner of the policy will be determined by the governance structure of both the library and its institution. The contact person would be anyone able to interpret, clarify, or answer questions about the policy.

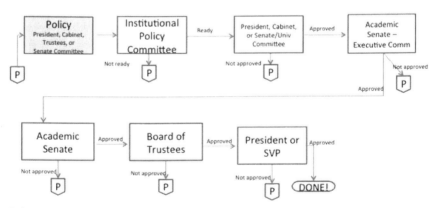

FIGURE 2.1
Sample Policy Approval Process for a University. *Allyson Mower.*

MAKING THE POLICY OFFICIAL

Whether revised or newly drafted, the next step will be internally vetting the document among colleagues and getting approval from appropriate governing bodies. To get a sense of what it might take to get your policy in place, here is a sample approval workflow for a large, public institution of higher learning:

Table 2.1. Sample Worksheet based on "Developing a Library Copyright Policy— An EIFL Guide"

Copyright Policy Drafting Worksheet
1. PURPOSE OF THE POLICY
2. STATEMENT OF LIBRARY'S ROLE AND MISSION
3. DEFINITIONS

4. POLICY
 	
  A. GENERAL RULES FOR LIBRARY EMPLOYEES
 	
  B. GENERAL RULES FOR LIBRARY USERS
 	
  C. PERMISSIONS

5. POLICY OWNER AND CONTACT

This may seem daunting, but it can go quickly once you get the conversations started. Knowing where to start can sometimes be the most time-consuming aspect. Not every institution or government entity will be as big, either, making the timeline more condensed, but you get the idea of the range of people that might need to be involved. Moreover, it also shows how crucial it is to have someone (yes, a dedicated librarian or library administrator) see the document through whatever process fits your library's context.

In their book *Implementing Public Policy*, Michael Hill and Peter Hupe consider policies to be "coping mechanisms," which is a good way of looking at something like a copyright policy.[1] Policies are a way of dealing with uncertainty and confusion, which, when it comes to copyright, can often produce both. Keep this general idea in mind as you go through the implementing process. Hill and Hupe also say that it is important to consider the amount of change required and the level of consensus in place at the time of implementation. A policy that requires little change and has a broad range of agreement with regard to its main goal and premise will have greater ease of becoming part of an institution's process or workflow. This means policies and their goals need to remain succinct and straightforward. If possible, have one goal per policy and get the goal agreed upon by a handful of library employees before any final votes by approval bodies and before implementation.

Once employees have reviewed the policy draft, the next step is to take the document to governing bodies outside the library, if applicable. Look back at your policy-drafting plan to determine who those entities are for your library's context. For city, municipal, county, tribal, or state libraries, that might be a library board, committee, or entity within the governor's office. If your library serves a federal agency, you would take the policy through the agency's governing structure. If you are in a federal agency library that has been outsourced, you would work with both the agency's internal governance as well as the outsourced company's governance, if needed.

General Steps for Library Policy Approval
1. Review by Library Employees
   a. Examples include:
      i. Library director
      ii. Library committee(s) or task force

2. Review by Non-Library Employees
   a. Examples include:
      i. Library board of trustees
      ii. School board
      iii. Institutional, school, or agency committee(s)
      iv. City, county, or tribal council(s)
      v. Executive offices (e.g., mayor, city manager, commissioner, governor, college president)

Most public agencies will have websites listing officers, committees, and contact information. Do some web searching to locate the websites relevant to your library's context. Then spend time looking through the websites to discover the preferred initial contact or process. For example, Salt Lake County in Utah has people submit an online request to review or draft a new policy. That would be one way of initiating contact with an entity representing the agency applicable to a county library. Library boards might also have a preferred method of working with representative entities. As the policy gets presented to the library board, the library director can ask (or maybe already knows) whom the policy would need to go to next, if at all. This would depend on whether your policy will impact what residents in city, county, or tribal areas can and cannot do when it comes to the use of copyrighted works.

Governance Process: State, City, County, Nonprofit, School, and Private Libraries

To help illustrate the possible variations in governance strategies for different types of libraries, the following section offers several governance examples. To locate the governance infrastructure for your library, consult the library's website and browse through meeting minutes and agendas.

State libraries typically have boards or commissions appointed by the governor for multi-year terms. Each board will have its own set of bylaws usually set by state law. Most boards govern policies and procedures, which library employees then implement. Each board will have a chair, and the chair (or secretary) will set the agenda. Typically, state library boards hire and review the library's director and hear reports from the director, so if you have a copyright policy idea and you are not the library director, bring up the topic with that person and ask how to have the item placed on the agenda. That is the case for the Texas State Library and Archives Commission, Iowa Commission of Libraries, and Maryland State Library. State library boards typically meet once a quarter or four times a year.

City and county libraries typically have boards of trustees to oversee the adoption of policies and procedures. Boards of trustees can have chairpersons or presidents to set the agenda. As with state library boards, city and county library boards will hire, review, and receive reports from the library director. How often the board meets is wholly dependent on the individual board itself and its bylaws. The Oxford Public Library Board in Oxford, Michigan, meets monthly as does the Auburn Public Library Board of Trustees in Auburn, Maine. The King County Law Library Board of Trustees in Washington state meets based on a schedule set by the board's secretary and does not post its meeting dates.

Libraries affiliated with nonprofit entities will also typically have a board that governs policies and procedures. Examples would include community, scientific or scholarly societies such as the YWCA, the Ecological Society of America, or the American Philosophical Society. Most nonprofits will have articles of incorporation that define the organization and its decision-making infrastructure, which usually includes a governing board. Like state, city, and county libraries, the governing board will have a president or chair that sets the agenda. Unlike state, city, and county libraries, a nonprofit board might not have a direct relationship with the library director, but will work closely with an executive director. A library employee within a nonprofit organization will want to work closely with the executive director on any policy approval and implementation. Like city and county library boards, the schedule of nonprofit board meetings is completely dependent on the board itself (as opposed to any state meeting laws) and its bylaws. Check the organization's main website to determine if a meeting schedule has been posted.

For school libraries, boards of education will review policies and procedures as specified in local and state education laws. The board is typically elected by voters in the district, and board members typically serve multi-year terms. Boards of education will have presidents or chairs that set the agenda. The frequency of meetings can vary. The Sauquoit Valley Central School Board of Education in Sauquoit, New York, meets twice a month. Other boards of education might only meet once a month. Like state, city, and county library boards, boards of education usually hire, review, and receive reports from the superintendent or chief school officer. Superintendents typically work with school principals, who work with teachers, librarians, and other school employees on policy development. A library director or media center manager within a school who needs to develop or implement a copyright policy would work closely with the school principal, who would then collaborate with the superintendent on interfacing with the board of education.

Universities, even though they are a type of school, do not normally have boards of education to oversee policies and procedures, but instead have boards of trustees. Multi-campus university systems typically have boards of regents who approve policies and procedures. Boards of trustees and regents will typically have chairpersons or presidents who set the agenda. Meeting frequency for university boards of trustees is monthly, for the most part, with university-system boards of regents meeting only once a quarter. Like state, city, county, and school library boards, university boards of trustees and regents will usually hire, review, and receive reports from the university president as well as the presiding officer representing the faculty.

Library directors or deans at universities looking to implement a copyright policy would want to work closely with both the university president and the presiding faculty officer to both implement and to interface with the board of trustees on policy approval. The flowchart included earlier in the chapter shows the process for policy approval at the University of Utah in Salt Lake City, Utah. It shows the process for getting a policy draft prepared for review by a board of trustees (and not a university-system board of regents). One good example of governance on a university-system level would be the University of California and its ten campuses.

Libraries within private corporations will operate within the institutional management infrastructure. For example, Halliburton Energy Solutions utilizes Halliburton Management System to establish business practices, policies, and code of conduct. This system gets managed by the corporation's law department. Corporate boards do not typically oversee policies and procedures for internal company operations, but instead oversee overall company performance for the benefit of shareholders. Corporate librarians looking to implement a copyright policy will need to work within the corporate structure.

No matter the governance process, policy drafters will want to have a clearly written and fully prepared policy to take to a board or executive officer for approval. Most board or commission members will not be experts in copyright. Assure board members that the draft has been written alongside relevant attorneys and informed by best practices in librarianship. The definitions section, if well crafted, will assist board and commission members in comprehending the elements of the document. Make certain the goal and scope of the policy are also clear, which will be achieved through close conversation with library employees.

Specific areas of librarianship most active within a library will become the main driver of what details to incorporate into a copyright policy. In chapter 3, we will spend time covering in more detail what elements of copyright will be most applicable within a policy based on library type.

NOTE

1. Hill, Michael; Hupe, Peter. *Implementing Public Policy*. Thousand Oaks, CA: SAGE Publications, 2002, 52–53.

3

Policy Drafting Based on Library Type

In this chapter, we will focus on drafting policies based on library type. As discussed in the last chapter, library type will affect what elements of copyright get included in the writing of the document and also impact how the policy will become official. This chapter will provide sample library mission statements from six types of libraries along with example copyright policies to illustrate both effective and ineffective approaches to copyright policy making.

The overarching difference in drafting a copyright policy based on library type comes down to how much direction types of employees might need to do their jobs. For example, based on the policies listed below, educators as a type of employee have been interpreted as needing specific and, at times, lengthy guidance on reuse of copyrighted content. Librarians and information professionals receive some guidance in the policies discussed below. City and county employees, students, local residents, tribal members, and web-based digital library users receive little to no guidance.

While some of the example policies are robust and others have the bare minimum or sometimes nothing at all, it does seem common that considering the reuse of copyrighted content in a library context comes at the end of a very long to-do list of other, general library operations, which is okay. As librarians and information professionals, we can give ourselves a little break (and a little reassurance) about the fact that our policies might be imperfect or even nonexistent. Focus, instead, on the positive aspects of policy making detailed previously: policies with clear goals in mind help reduce confusion and uncertainty and can, perhaps, even help create efficiency.

At whatever point within your copyright policy making or revising makes sense, then proceed within that time frame. If you find yourself frequently answering copyright questions, looking up the information each time, sending a different answer depending on who is asking, or having to often say that you are not certain what the approach should be, then it might be a good time to consider implementing or revising a copyright policy for your library.

As you begin, use the library types below to get more specific guidance. If you are not certain what type of library you work in, if you work within a library that combines several types, or if your library type is not included, then simply use the drafting template and copyright definitions available in chapters 1 and 2.

School Libraries

The National School Library standards released by the American Association of School Libraries (AASL) in November 2018 offer new and bold approaches to learning and information literacy that have exciting implications for copyright policies and workflows in libraries. The standards take a nuanced and individualized orientation by focusing on creating, thinking, and growing. One example the association provides is of a student using a 3-D printer to express an abstract concept she had read in a novel.[1] Having a 3-D printer and encouraging its use would necessitate a copyright policy. A policy would help define both reuse guidelines as well as ownership of the file and printed object. It would also help users know what the library would be responsible for in terms of print failures or mistakes.

The standards address other copyright-related areas such as innovating, creating, and sharing. Shirley Simmons, assistant superintendent of educational services for the Norman Public School District, says that the National School Library standards address how librarians, teachers, and students "approach learning and interact with content."[2] Activities surrounding these concepts would have a direct relationship with copyright.

If a school library planned to incorporate these new standards into library services, then revising or creating a new copyright policy would be a useful activity to go alongside of it, especially if the mission or vision statement changed because of the new standards. If the new standards are not yet being implemented, then working alongside the existing mission or vision statement will provide an easy starting point.

For example, the mission of the library at the Mt. Pleasant School in Rolla, North Dakota, is "To Open the Doors of the Past, Present, and Future," an excellent mission.[3] The mission of the school is "Learning Today to Prepare for Tomorrow," and the vision is "to provide a stimulating learning environment across the curriculum, maximizing individual student potential and ensuring that students of all abilities are prepared to meet future challenges."[4] Both are great missions and visions to operate from.

The library serves 247 K–12 students and has one librarian. There is no indication that the library serves the school's teachers or administrators. The library's Copyright Policy indicates that copyright notices are placed by copiers and computers throughout the school. It also states that students will not plagiarize and that library employees do not copy media. The policy appears to apply primarily to students, but does at times mention teachers. The document provides a bulleted list under a general heading of "Some material may be used under Fair Use laws."[5]

The list consists of details from what has come to be called educational fair use guidelines. The guidelines—originally called "Agreement on Guidelines for Classroom Copying in Not-for-Profit Educational Institutions with respect to books and periodicals"—were created in 1976 by a congressional ad hoc group consisting of lawmakers, authors, and publishers.[6] The agreement distinguished between a teacher's copying when doing his or her own research to prepare for teaching and making multiple copies for distribution to students in the teacher's classroom. The guidelines were not developed with students in mind, nor were they intended to replace the broader allowances described in the Fair Use exception, Section 107.

Much of the library's policy comes from the section of the guidelines about making multiple copies for students in a teacher's classroom. This could potentially be confusing for a student enrolled at Mt. Pleasant School in Rolla, North Dakota. It is probably unlikely that a student would thoroughly consult the lengthy list, so it is possible the document might not provide the right type of guidance for a student. It could also potentially be confusing for the librarian at the school, who might have a difficult time remembering all the allowances on the list when in the crux of helping a student navigate a research topic for a class assignment.

Given the library's broad and open mission, the copyright policy might be too narrow. The policy could simply state a commitment to compliance with the Copyright Act and that students will cite all sources and not include the lengthy and confusing list meant for teachers. This would allow the librarian to more easily help students focus on learning and meeting the goals of both the library and the school. A separate policy could be made at the district level that focuses on what teachers, as district employees, can do when making copies for the classroom.

This is the approach that Nissitissit Middle School in Pepperell, Maine, took. The library's Copyright Policy applies to teachers and staff only. The mission of the library is "to ensure that students and staff are effective users of ideas and information."[7] The mission of the school is to "recognize the unique needs of the middle school student while providing a safe and respectful learning environment."[8] Both are excellent missions, like Mt. Pleasant's. Because the mission of the library has a broad base, the copyright policy could be expanded to include rules for students since the mission statement also includes students. The rules for teachers could also potentially be made broader to allow for more decision-making on the part of teachers and other staff. If the goal of the library is to have librarians teach staff how to effectively use ideas and information, involving them in the ethics surrounding reuse and the creation of new works could be a powerful learning opportunity.

Louisville Catholic Schools in Louisville, Kentucky, took a somewhat broader approach with its copyright policy. The mission of the library is to serve "as the center for educational research and as a resource for teachers, students, and parents in achieving curriculum outcomes."[9] The mission of Louisville Catholic Schools is to "provide a unique environment that allows students to grow in their faith while performing at high academic levels."[10] The policy includes both fair use principles, which they have applied to educators only, and also incorporates educational fair use guidelines as a teacher fact sheet. This approach could allow some flexibility for personal teaching style, which seems useful and effective. And while the mission of the library includes students and parents, the copyright policy only pertains to teachers. Incorporating the fair use exception on the whole instead of the principles and fact sheets could make the policy relevant to all patrons of the library.

The common theme throughout these school library examples is the desire to guide teachers as employees. The school libraries represented here (and represented in the National School Library Standards) have the overarching and conceptual goal of opening minds, educating, and instructing library users about information reuse, but the practical component, essentially, is relaying to teachers how much they can copy and distribute without permission. An element to keep in mind when crafting a copyright policy for a school library is the fact that the use of copyrighted works in the educational process is crucial. Having clearly defined rules that allow for both flexibility and clarity for teachers and students will make the work of meeting educational missions, including the work of librarians and information professionals, more successful.

A copyright policy in a school library could go beyond the employee-only focus to also provide guidance to students on what it means to copy a work to comment on or critique for cultural or scholarly purposes. Let the policy facilitate students in their learning process to see the possibilities based on the broader purpose of copyright and then drill down on specifics like the fair use exception or obtaining permission. One element to consider for a copyright policy in a school (or academic) library is distinguishing between plagiarism, privacy, and copyright. Plagiarism is an academic standard defined by ethical principles of citation and attribution that usually get spelled out in local policies and student handbooks. Privacy, while a legal concept, is defined by local laws and some federal laws such as the Privacy Act, the Health Insurance Portability and Accountability Act, and Family Educational Rights and Privacy Act. And, as we have seen in this book, copyright is a federal law governing the rights and exceptions surrounding eligible works of authorship.

Academic Libraries

In its 2018 revision of Standards for Libraries in Higher Education, the Association of College & Research Libraries (ACRL) highlighted intellectual property in its professional values statement: "Libraries advance professional values of intellectual freedom, intellectual property rights and values, user privacy and confidentiality, collaboration, and user-centered service."[11] The performance indicator within the stated principle includes "[balancing] between the interests of information users and those of rights holders through policy and educational programming." These two statements bring copyright policy-making to the forefront.

The revised standards also emphasize campus partnerships and external relations. A copyright policy within the library that focused on "information users" would require an engagement with the information users the library serves, which would include students, staff, and faculty. If a copyright policy within a library only guides library employees, then the level of engagement with partners outside the library would be limited to the institution's attorneys.

For example, the mission of the University of California Libraries is to "provide information resources and services to UC faculty, students, and staff in direct support of the University of California's teaching, learning, research, patient care, and public service goals."[12] The mission of the University of California is to "serve society as a center of higher learning, providing long-term societal benefits through transmitting advanced knowledge, discovering new knowledge, and functioning as an active working repository of organized knowledge."[13] The copyright policy for the institution is a broad, fair use-only policy that applies to faculty, staff, and students with a specific reference to employees and the university's role in defending employees "who acted within the scope of their University employment and who made use of the copyrighted work at issue in an informed, reasonable, and good faith manner."[14] The policy does not mention other exemptions such as Section 108 Libraries & Archives or Section 110(1) Face-to-Face Teaching, but it states that Section 107 Fair Use applies to both employees and students in the context of the university's mission. This is clearly a campus-based policy and not simply a library-only policy. A librarian or information professional could have initiated the creation and passage of the policy as a campus partnership, but it impacts more than librarians and information professionals working within a single University of California campus.

The University System of Georgia (USG) utilizes a similar approach by focusing their policy on the fair use exception. The policy does not incorporate Section 108 Libraries & Archives and only briefly mentions Section 110(1) Face-to-Face Teaching. This is probably based on the system's mission to "providing the highest quality undergraduate and graduate education to students; pursuing leading-edge basic and applied research, scholarly inquiry, and creative endeavors; and bringing intellectual resources to the citizenry."[15] Each university and college within the system has its own mission, and each library at those colleges and universities also has its own mission. For example, the mission of the library at Georgia State University is to "[p]rovide resources and services that enhance student learning and success, inspire creative expression, enable the creation of new knowledge and facilitate informed dialogue."[16] The University of Georgia Library has a separate mission "to advance the [University of Georgia's] mission by providing the best possible access to recorded knowledge, actively contribute to the success of students and faculty through teaching and research services provided in physical and virtual environments that enhance learning and intellectual creativity, and exemplify the University's strategic priority to serve the citizens of Georgia and beyond."[17] The differing mission statements help delineate the audiences that will be impacted by a copyright policy. The overarching mission for USG focuses on impacting students, faculty, and citizens, which you can see reflected in their copyright policy.

The University of Oklahoma uses a single mission statement for its system and campuses, which is to "provide the best possible educational experience for our students through excellence in teaching, research and creative activity, and service to the state and society."[18] The institution has a general copyright statement that focuses on electronic publications distributed through the institution's web servers. The statement requires evidence of permission from rights holders and mentions fair use only when "restricted use of copyright materials" is made.[19] The library has its own policy to govern its course reserve service and places an emphasis on evidence of permission or licensing. The policy does allow for a reliance on Section 107 Fair Use by indicating that a "small proportion of the total assigned reading for a particular course" is allowed by a professor at the institution.[20] The policy references only a single subsection of Section 108 Libraries & Archives. It does not include other subsections of Section 108 for librarians and information professionals working in areas other than course reserves, such as preservation or interlibrary loan.

Like school librarians, academic librarians who initiate copyright policies will need to establish a clear audience for the policy by simply answering this question: Is this for library employees only or is this also for educators, researchers, and students? Knowing a little bit about this question will help determine if the policy is internal to the library or if it is external and needs to go beyond the library to the wider college or university community.

City and County Libraries

When it comes to drafting a copyright policy, the primary difference between a school or academic library and a city, county, or state library is the presence and type of employee, for example, teachers as paid employees.

School districts and academic institutions employ educators to fulfill their missions, so copyright policies tend to be geared toward teachers and the teaching activity. City, county, and state governments employ a range of workers, but typically not teachers, at least not directly. Moreover, libraries that fall within a city, county, or state jurisdiction usually focus on developing policies that apply to library users from the general public and, at times, library employees, but generally not other employees within that city, county, or state governmental entity.

For example, the mission of West Chester Public Library in West Chester, Pennsylvania, is to serve as a "destination for connection, collaboration, and enrichment through knowledge and community engagement."[21] One of West Chester Public Library's goals in relation to this mission is to provide "opportunities to read, learn, and create."[22] The library's copyright policy pertains only to library employees and volunteers and has the general goal of compliance. It allows employees and volunteers to copy based on specific exemptions in the Copyright Act. This seems like a very straightforward approach to communicating general compliance, but it places the onus on employees and volunteers to know the exemptions and read them for themselves. This could be a good strategy in terms of encouraging librarians and information professionals in educating themselves in the language of the statute, but the policy drafting could incorporate some specifics, especially from Section 108 Libraries & Archives, as a time-saving mechanism for library employees. The policy does not mention patron or library user behavior. Given the library's mission to support the community in their creation of new knowledge, the policy could be expanded to include the general population.

Chicago Public Library in Chicago, Illinois, has a similar mission of supporting residents in their pursuit of reading, lifelong learning, and discovery of new information.[23] Their mission statement does not use the word "create," however, as West Chester Public Library does, but much of the library's programming focuses on encouraging residents to create. The library's copyright policy provides some guidance for patrons by mentioning that determining exceptions or obtaining permission is the patron's responsibility. Primarily, the policy communicates to rights holders ways to issue a takedown notice if a copyrighted work is found in one of the library's digital collections. The policy also includes elements of Section 108 Libraries & Archives, but the policy does not indicate that those elements apply to library employees. With a few distinct headings, the policy could become clearer for library employees. And by adding more references to various exceptions, it could provide more guidance for library patrons.

Auburn Public Library in Auburn, Maine, includes patrons in their copyright policy by including a specific reference to Section 107 Fair Use and providing direction to get permission when copying a work would replace a sale of a work. The policy has a section on copy machines and printers and a section for library staff. The guidance for library employees is very minimal and focuses only on compliance. It refers librarians and information professionals to an ALA fact sheet, but does not list any components of Section 108 Libraries & Archives and how library employees should implement the exception. The mission of Auburn Public Library is to bring "people, resources and ideas together to engage, enlighten and enrich community."[24] One of the library's goals is to foster a culture of innovation within the library and within the community. The patron section in the library's copyright policy supports this goal, but the portion for library employees would need additional information to more fully support this component of the library's mission.

The Public Library Association has organized several exciting initiatives and projects, many of which will coincide with copyright. A city library that plans to implement initiatives such as digital literacy, family engagement, and/or creative community connections might want to consider having more detailed copyright policies. Through any of these initiatives, both patrons and library employees would engage with copyrighted content, either through publishing and distribution ventures such as online blogging or the short story dispenser to the public performance of books in the Every Child Ready to Read program.[25] Knowing how much copyrighted content can be used without permission and ways in which to obtain permission would provide much-needed guidance that a policy could help provide. As city librarians draft and implement detailed copyright policies related to these initiatives, the process will place them in communication with the library board, serving as an active way of engaging with the board on exciting and timely library services and programming.

As with city libraries, county libraries have a range of mission statements and approaches to policies. For example, Somerset County Library System in New Jersey has a mission to partner with "residents to connect, to explore, to share and to discover."[26] The operative term in this mission statement is "resident," which gets defined as "people in Somerset County [who want to] expand their knowledge and talents, make informed decisions, enrich their leisure hours, and enhance their daily lives."[27] The mentioning of leisure time and daily life make this library distinct from, say, a school library that focuses on meeting specific curriculum needs, primarily for students, but also for employees. Somerset County Library's policy on copyright is limited to compliance only as listed in Section D of the Collection Management Policy. While this approach does not provide guidance for library employees, it is sufficient in terms of supporting the library's mission to serve residents.

The Jefferson County Library in Jefferson County, Missouri, has a slightly more robust approach to copyright policy. Aspects of copyright get incorporated into the library's interlibrary loan policy, which provides quite a bit of guidance for library employees. Copyright also gets included in the library's public services content creation policy, which is oriented to patrons. The policy requires that patrons obtain permission from copyright holders when "transmitting or reproducing copyrighted or patented content" when using the library's "public media and maker resources."[28] According to their mission statement, "Jefferson County Library is where our community learns, connects, and turns dreams into reality."[29]

County librarians, like city librarians, can use the policy-making process to engage directly with the board of trustees. The process can serve as an opportunity to highlight emerging initiatives within the library that directly impact the community that also relate to copyright.

State Libraries

State libraries differ from school, academic, city, and county libraries in their focus on serving other libraries within their state boundaries. Many serve patrons directly, but on a less regular basis in comparison to city and county libraries. They can be somewhat similar to school and academic libraries in that they directly serve employees. While school and academic libraries primarily support teachers as a kind of employee, state libraries serve those employed by the state, which can represent a range of types of employees from legislative analysts to attorneys to public policy managers. Rebecca Gerber defines state libraries as agencies that support

> the work of the legislature and other state employees [and] typically maintain a collection of state publications, works by local authors, and local publications,

such as newsletters. State libraries serve as the State Library Administrative Agencies, the official agencies charged by law with the extension and development of library services under the Grants to States program of the Institute of Museum and Library Services (IMLS). They are located in each of the 50 states and the District of Columbia, U.S. Territories (Guam, American Samoa, the Commonwealth of Puerto Rico, the Commonwealth of the Northern Mariana Islands, and the U.S. Virgin Islands), and the Freely Associated States (Federated States of Micronesia, Republic of Palau, and the Republic of the Marshall Islands).[30]

For example, the Texas State Library and Archives Commission has the following mission areas:

- Preserving the archival record of Texas (Archives and Information Services)
- Enhancing the service capacity of Texas public, academic, and school libraries (Library Development and Networking)
- Assisting public agencies in the maintenance of their records (State and Local Records Management)
- Meeting the reading needs of Texans with disabilities (Talking Book Program)[31]

The copyright policy for Texas State Library and Archives Commission resides within the Texas Interlibrary Loan Protocol. The policy is geared towards other libraries and not to any individual user. It is a compliance policy that references both Section 107 Fair Use and Section 108 Libraries & Archives, but provides no particular details on these exceptions. It encourages Texas libraries utilizing the service to consider guidelines such as the Commission on New Technological Uses of Copyrighted Works (CONTU) and fair use for educators and librarians. These guidelines do not get spelled out, however, only referenced.[32] Given the commission's preservation mission, having a standalone policy detailing the nine subsections of Section 108 Libraries & Archives would provide state library employees with solid guidance.

Another example is the Maryland State Library, which provides "strategic leadership, resources, and programmatic support to Maryland libraries to transform lives."[33] Like Texas State Library and Archives Commission, the Maryland State Library also provides library services to the blind. They also administer the Deaf Culture Digital Library. Maryland State Library's copyright policy is a fair use policy that primarily applies to their website visitors; the policy does not provide any guidance to library employees.[34] Expanding the media policies to also include guidance for library employees could provide additional support.

The State Library of Iowa could also consider adding to their existing copyright policy. The mission of the State Library of Iowa is to "[strengthen] Iowa libraries and information access for Iowans."[35] State Library of Iowa's copyright policy is a takedown policy in line with its Iowa Publications Online service. Since the mission is broad, an additional copyright policy that incorporates Section 107 Fair Use and Section 108 Libraries & Archives could assist librarians and information professionals working within the institution as well as Iowans who utilize state library services.

California State Library focuses their copyright policy on reuse by referencing Section 107 Fair Use to govern its patrons. The policy does not reference Section 108 Libraries & Archives, nor does it provide guidance for library employees. The policy requires that users "determine the copyright status of any material provided by the library." The policy indicates that "the library can claim only physical ownership," which is correct, but the policy also requires patrons to seek their library's permission when publishing the works, the basis of which is not clear.[36] Like other state libraries, California State Library has a broad mission to "[empower . . .] the nation's most diverse and populous state."[37] Preservation is a component of their mission area and, as such, their copyright policy could be expanded to include Section 108 Libraries & Archives.

Given state libraries' general missions to serve state employees and other librarians and libraries within their area, the primary focus for a copyright policy would be library employees. More clarity might be needed to show what library employees can copy for preservation purposes or when fulfilling an interlibrary loan/document delivery request. A state library could also consider working with a state attorney on reuse and permission guidelines for state employees.

A state librarian, as with city, county, school, and academic librarians, could use the policy-making process as a chance to engage with the library's governance board in a meaningful way. Policy drafting and revising in the copyright context could also open up dialogue between state librarians and other state employees to ensure that library services and collections are sufficiently tailored to their information needs.

Tribal Libraries

Sandra Littletree recently defined tribal libraries as libraries that "are planned and administered by a tribe, pueblo, village, or native group [. . . that] incorporate and reflect Native lifeways and perspectives into their services, collections, policies, and design."[38] For example, the Ute Indian Tribe's Venita K. Taveapont Memorial Library follows this definition; its mission is to become an integral part of the tribe by encouraging lifelong learning and Ute authorship.

The library utilizes Section 107 Fair Use in its policy to guide patrons, but does not reference Section 108 Libraries & Archives, nor does it focus on the work of library employees. Based on the library's mission to increase storytelling and authorship, the policy could potentially be expanded (or a separate policy created) to provide guidance on ownership and reuse of indigenous knowledge.

Special Libraries

Special libraries provide specific and tailored services to a distinct population such as those working within a private corporation or a nonprofit institution. This means missions can vary across special libraries. For example, the Ecological Society of America, the Botanical Society of America, the Society for the Study of Evolution, and the Society for Economic Botany have partnered to establish the LifeDiscoveryEd Digital Library as a nonprofit, special library.

The library's mission is to provide "a platform for scientists and educators to locate and contribute peer reviewed resources for 21st century undergraduate ecology education. [The Digital Library] strives to foster a community of ecology education users and contributors."[39] The library's copyright policy utilizes a Creative Commons license to guide library patrons on how works in the digital library can be used.

This range of library types shows how vastly different copyright policies get incorporated. Some policies provide in-depth guidance, and others offer only basic copyright information. School and academic libraries tend to have policies geared toward teachers and, at times, incorrectly apply teacher guidelines to students. School and academic library copyright policies rarely provide guidance to library employees, representing an area of possible revision and improvement. City, county, state, and tribal libraries have a mixture of patron and employee-focused copyright policies. Some offer direction only to patrons, while others only mention librarians and information professionals. Some of them address the library-as-publisher mission by utilizing takedown policies. The one special library example demonstrated in more detail the publishing role that many digital libraries take on, which requires a different type of policy geared more toward obtaining permission to publish original content.

By looking into a library's mission statement and thinking about its broader context and audience, copyright policy drafters can easily tailor the purpose and definitions of the policy to ensure that it remains relevant. Much of the work comes in knowing that copyright consists of many exceptions. Working with local attorneys to understand which exceptions apply to the area and people your library serves will make for a strong and useful policy. In the next chapter, we will explore how to implement elements of a copyright policy into a daily library workflow.

NOTES

1. American Association of School Libraries. "New National School Library Standards Encourage Students to Explore, Collaborate, Engage." *District Administration* (September 2018). https://standards.aasl.org/wp-content/uploads/2018/08/0918_AASL_DAadvertorial_pages.pdf.

2. Ibid.

3. Mt. Pleasant School Library. Accessed June 3, 2019. https://www.mt-pleasant.k12.nd.us/apps/pages/index.jsp?uREC_ID=397297&type=d.

4. Mt. Pleasant School District. "About Us." Accessed June 3, 2019. https://www.mt-pleasant.k12.nd.us/apps/pages/index.jsp?uREC_ID=392653&type=d.

5. Mt. Pleasant School Library. "Copyright Policy." Accessed June 3, 2019. http://www.mt-pleasant.k12.nd.us/library/copyright-policy.

6. U.S. Copyright Office. "Circular 21: Reproduction of Copyrighted Works by Educators and Librarians." Washington, DC: Library of Congress (August 2014): 5. https://www.copyright.gov/circs/circ21.pdf.

7. North Middlesex Regional School District. "Library." Accessed June 3, 2019. http://nms.nmrsd.org/library.

8. Nissitissit Middle School. "Mission Statement and Core Values." Accessed June 3, 2019. http://nms.nmrsd.org/aboutnms.

9. Archdiocese of Louisville. "Library Media Guidelines," 3. Accessed June 3, 2019. http://louisvillecatholicschools.com/wp-content/uploads/2017/01/LibraryMediaGuidelines.pdf.

10. Louisville Catholic Schools. "Why Choose Catholic Schools." Accessed June 4, 2019. https://louisvillecatholicschools.com/join-us/choose-catholic-schools/.

11. Association of College & Research Libraries. "Standards for Libraries in Higher Education." Accessed June 24, 2019. http://www.ala.org/acrl/standards/standardslibraries.

12. University of California Libraries. "Vision and Priorities." Accessed June 4, 2019. https://libraries.universityofcalifornia.edu/about/vision-and-priorities.

13. University of California Office of the President. "UC's Mission." Accessed June 4, 2019. https://www.ucop.edu/uc-mission/index.html.

14. University of California. "Copyright and fair use." Accessed June 4, 2019. http://copyright.universityofcalifornia.edu/resources/copyright-fair-use.html.

15. University System of Georgia. "Copyright Policy." Accessed June 4, 2019. https://www.usg.edu/copyright/.

16. Georgia State University Library. "Mission, Vision, and Values." Accessed June 4, 2019. https://library.gsu.edu/home/about-the-library/about/welcome/mission/.

17. University of Georgia Library. "Welcome from the University Librarian." Accessed June 4, 2019. https://www.libs.uga.edu/administration/.

18. University of Oklahoma. "Public Affairs." Accessed June 14, 2019. http://www.ou.edu/publicaffairs.

19. University of Oklahoma. "Copyright." Accessed June 14, 2019. http://www.ou.edu/publicaffairs/mediacenter/copyright.

20. University of Oklahoma Libraries. "Copyright & Reserves." Accessed June 14, 2019. https://libraries.ou.edu/content/copyright-reserves.

21. West Chester Public Library. "2015–2020 Strategic Plan," 2. Accessed June 4, 2019. https://wcpubliclibrary.org/wp-content/uploads/WCPL-Strategic-Plan-2015-2020.pdf.

22. Ibid.

23. Chicago Public Library. "About Us." Accessed June 14, 2019. https://www
.chipublib.org/about-us/.

24. Auburn Public Library. "About the Library." Accessed June 14, 2019. http://
www.auburnpubliclibrary.org/about-the-library/.

25. Public Library Association. "PLA Initiatives and Projects." Accessed June 25,
2019. http://www.ala.org/pla/initiatives.

26. Somerset County Library System. "Policies." Accessed June 14, 2019. https://
sclsnj.org/using-our-libraries/policies/.

27. Somerset County Library System. "Operating Policies, Collection Management
Policy," 1. Accessed June 14, 2019. https://s40873y1pyb1ozqsg275sisu-wpengine
.netdna-ssl.com/wp-content/uploads/M-Collection-Management-Policy.pdf.

28. Jefferson County Library. "Library Policies and Procedures: Library Designated
Forum for Content Creation Policy." Accessed June 14, 2019. https://www.jeffcolib
.org/about-us/library-policies-and-guidelines.

29. Jefferson County Library. "Mission and History." Accessed June 14, 2019.
https://www.jeffcolib.org/about-us/our-mission.

30. Gerber, Rebecca. "State Library Agencies." Accessed June 25, 2019. http://
libguides.ala.org/state-libraries.

31. Texas State Library and Archives Commission. "About Us." Accessed June 21,
2019. https://www.tsl.texas.gov/about.

32. Texas State Library and Archives Commission. "Texas Interlibrary Loan
Protocol." Accessed June 21, 2019. https://www.tsl.texas.gov/texshare/illprot.html.

33. Maryland State Library. "About Maryland State Library." Accessed June 21,
2019. https://www.marylandlibraries.org/Pages/About-MSL.aspx.

34. Maryland State Library. "Media Policies and Branding Information." Accessed
June 21, 2019. https://www.marylandlibraries.org/Pages/Media-Policies-and
-Branding.aspx.

35. State Library of Iowa. "Mission." Accessed June 21, 2019. https://www
.statelibraryofiowa.org/about/stmt/mission.

36. California State Library. "Copyright Policy." Accessed June 21, 2019. http://
www.library.ca.gov/california-history/fair-use/.

37. California State Library. "Mission and Values." Accessed June 21, 2019. http://
www.library.ca.gov/about/mission/.

38. Littletree, Sandra. "'Let Me Tell You about Indian Libraries': Self-Determination,
Leadership, and Vision: The Basis of Tribal Library Development in the United
States." Ann Arbor, MI: ProQuest Dissertations & Theses Global, 2019, 57.

39. EcoEd Digital Library. "About EcoEd Digital Library." Accessed June 21, 2019.
https://ecoed.esa.org/EcoEdDL_About.

4

Incorporating the Policy into Daily Work

In this chapter, we will look at ways to incorporate a copyright policy into daily work at a library so that it will become a document that actually gets used. Actively using the policy on a regular basis will make the professional duties of librarians more efficient, effective, and consistent. With the objectives and goals already defined, a policy can quickly and easily become part of an everyday workflow for librarians and information professionals. Anyone working in document delivery can use it, anyone on a service desk, whoever produces advertising for a library, those who create digital collections, those who partner with teachers on content delivery for students, and librarians who provide instruction. Imagine being able to offer a definitive response for your own situation (or someone you are helping) that incorporates the full range of exceptions within the copyright system. Whenever you wonder how much you can copy or what you can tell a patron about how much can be copied, you can automatically turn to the policy for immediate guidance.

The easiest way to incorporate the policy into a regular workflow is to keep the policy nearby and familiarize yourself with it. Print it out if you need to and keep it on your desk. Post it to your office wall. Or, if the library's policies get posted online, keep it open in your web browser and bookmark it. Know the policy's name or number or whatever nomenclature gets used by your library, school, or institution. Whenever you find yourself in a situation that involves copying a work of authorship or publicly distributing, performing, or displaying it, consult your policy. It will become more and more familiar to you as you do your daily work, and eventually you will be able to answer the question without having to look at the policy!

The language of the policy will provide details about which rules to follow, but it only serves as one component of the overall document. The other aspect will include procedures, workflows, and forms. Sometimes procedures get incorporated into the policy document itself, and sometimes they remain separate. This chapter also includes sample procedures that can easily be integrated with a copyright policy. Workflows will help ensure that the library employees or library users who are expected to adhere to a policy can do so without too much burden or confusion. This chapter also suggests possible wording for forms as well as a potential training curriculum to further assist in integrating a policy into everyday work situations.

It will be important to keep in mind that applying the policy will be relevant to different areas of the library or institution depending on how a work of authorship is being used. For example, if a teacher asks a librarian if she can use a DVD from the library's collection to play in class, the policy would provide the answer simply based on the face-to-face teaching exception. If the teacher then also wanted to show the movie at a special event outside of class, the policy would indicate that the face-to-face teaching exception does not cover public performances outside of the curriculum and classroom. Because of this, the policy would then indicate that permission from the rights holder would be needed, and the librarian could provide guidance on ways in which the teacher can obtain public performance permission. The teacher may be the same, but her two uses are different in the scheme of the core rights of copyright.

Let us say the same teacher also asked the librarian to make a copy of the film and post it on the library's server so that students could watch it on their own time outside of class. The policy would indicate that Section 110(1) is only an exception that applies to public performance and display and does not cover copying and distributing. The policy would provide guidance on obtaining permission or, if set up in the policy, conducting a Section 107 Fair Use evaluation since, as we saw earlier, fair use applies to the right to copy. Again, same teacher, but different set of activities in the realm of the core rights.

Similarly, perhaps a patron wants to print a work of authorship using the library's 3-D printer. If the library has a fair use policy to guide patrons on personal copying of copyrighted works, the librarian or information professional overseeing the service would need evidence of permission or licensing. Permissions and licensing would become relevant if a library has a fair use policy because, in the process of 3-D printing, an entire digital file gets downloaded and reused, which would make it difficult for a patron to adhere to the library's policy. Recall the definition of Section 107 Fair Use from chapter 1 which states that copying needs to be brief and only for purposes of comment, criticism, news reporting, teaching, research, and scholarship. The policy would need to include a definition of fair use and also include brief procedures regarding permissions. An example of this can be seen in Auburn Public Library's copyright policy (full policy available in chapter 5) and in the example wording for a 3-D printing form provided later in the chapter.

The service point in the library dedicated to 3-D printing could ask patrons in-person or through a form to provide evidence of permission or licensing when using the printer. Together, these elements would guide patrons on how they can utilize works of authorship within the library and on library-issued equipment and technology. It would become an information literacy moment to educate library patrons about the reuse of someone else's work and help them stay within the expectations of the library's copyright policy.

From these examples, we can see how a copyright policy can be applied to various settings and situations a librarian or information professional may face in a library. How much the policy will address procedures and workflows will be entirely dependent on preference. The basic workflows shown in the next section could potentially be incorporated into a procedures section. Workflows could also stand outside with only a reference in the policy.

POSSIBLE WORKFLOWS, FORMS, AND TRAINING PROGRAMS TO ASSOCIATE WITH A COPYRIGHT POLICY

This section offers suggestions on how to fully embed a copyright policy into a library's operations. Librarians and information professionals can adopt various procedures, workflows, forms, and educational programming that will assist both fellow employees as well as library patrons. The first part of the section includes possible workflows related to some of the more popular exceptions relevant to libraries: Section 107 Fair Use, Section 108 Libraries & Archives, Section 110(1) Face-to-Face Teaching. The section then discusses details on developing a library-based permission form for the purpose of getting permission from a rights holder to publish original content if that becomes a relevant service point at a library. This would be applicable to librarians and information professionals who develop digital collections or digital libraries, or who oversee publishing programs. Wording for a 3-D printing service form is included, and a brief listing of possible educational programming or training curriculum is also considered.

The following sample workflows could be incorporated into a policy or simply used in day-to-day library operations. The workflows are ordered based on the numbering of the exception, as detailed in previous chapters.

Section 107 Fair Use Workflow

Step 1. Check U.S. Copyright Office Registration Records

Examine the work for author and/or publisher to determine rights holder.

Step 2. Search for Availability of Permissions

Use the title, author, rights holder to search for permissions. For books, journals, and other serials, check Copyright Clearance Center (CCC). For movies, check studio websites. For songs, check music rights management websites. For images, check artists' websites or CCC.

Step 3. Determine General Availability of the Work

Search the library catalog, book vendor site, general web.

Step 4. Conduct Fair Use Evaluation

Using results from the market research, use the American Library Association's Fair Use Evaluator (see chapter 1) or Columbia University Library's Fair Use Checklist (included below).

Table 4.1. Purpose of the Use

Favoring Fair Use	Opposing Fair Use
❏ Teaching (including multiple copies for classroom use) ❏ Research & scholarship ❏ Nonprofit educational institution ❏ Criticism, comment, news reporting ❏ Transformative (changes the work for new utility) ❏ Parody	❏ Commercial activity ❏ Profiting from the use ❏ Entertainment ❏ Bad-faith behavior ❏ Using a work intended as instructional media

Table 4.2. Nature of the Work

Favoring Fair Use	Opposing Fair Use
❏ Published work ❏ Factual or nonfiction based	❏ Unpublished work ❏ Highly creative work (fiction, art, music, film, play)

Table 4.3. Amount to Be Used

Favoring Fair Use	Opposing Fair Use
❏ Small quantity ❏ Portion used is not central or significant to the entire work ❏ Amount is appropriate for favored educational purpose	❏ All or large portion of work is used ❏ Portion is central to or "heart of the work"

Table 4.4. Effect on the Market for the Work

Favoring Fair Use	Opposing Fair Use
❏ User owns lawfully purchased or acquired copy of original work ❏ Permission or licensing mechanism not available	❏ Could replace sale of the work ❏ Permission or licensing available

Source: Columbia University Library Copyright Advisory Office. Attribution: Kenneth D. Crews, formerly of Columbia University, and Dwayne K. Buttler, University of Louisville. Used under the terms of the Creative Commons Attribution License.

Section 108 Libraries & Archives Workflow

Step 1. Eligibility

Act within the scope of your library employment. Direct or indirect commercial advantage is not allowed. Place copyright notices at appropriate service points.

Step 2. Copyright Expiration

When receiving a request to copy, quickly examine the work for copyright eligibility or expiration. If uncertain, follow these additional steps:

Step 2a. Authorship If eligible for copyright protection, determine who created the work and research his or her life and death dates. Note this information in workflow software. If the author is unknown, mark it as orphan for further decision-making.

Step 2b. Publication Status and Date   Determine the publication status and date of the work. When were copies of the work made available to the general public (for sale or for free)?

Step 2c. Copyright Notice   If published, examine the work for a © notice.

Step 2d. Copyright Registration and Renewal   If published before 1989, determine if the rights holder registered and renewed the work.

Step 2e. Determine Expiration   Use the American Library Association's Public Domain Slider (see chapter 1) to determine expiration using the details gathered in the previous steps.

Step 3. For Lending, Make Isolated Copies and Check Borrowing Records

If staffing is available, library personnel can make isolated and unrelated copies of a copyrighted work to fulfill a request. Search records of filled loan requests to determine that the library did not receive more than five articles published in the same journal within the last five years.

Step 4. For Borrowing, Verify Borrowing Library

Ask the borrowing library if it has verified on its order form that the request conforms to the Copyright Act.

Step 5. For Reserve, Conduct Fair Use Evaluations and No Consumables

The Reserve desk can make and circulate a copy of a copyrighted work based on Section 107 Fair Use, but cannot copy works intended for instruction such as workbooks and standardized tests.

Step 6. For Preservation, Determine Publication Status and Search for New Work

Determine the publication status and date of the work. Were copies of the work made available to the general public (for sale or for free)? If not, work is unpublished and a copy can be made for preservation or deposit in another library. If published, search for a new work before copying for preservation.

Section 110(1) Face-to-Face Teaching Workflow

To fully understand this workflow, let us look at the exact wording of the face-to-face teaching exception in the Copyright Act:

performance or display of a work by instructors or pupils in the course of face-to-face teaching activities of a nonprofit educational institution, in a classroom or similar place devoted to instruction, unless, in the case of a motion picture or other audiovisual work, the performance, or the display of individual images, is given by means of a copy that was not lawfully made under this title, and that the person responsible for the performance knew or had reason to believe was not lawfully made;[1]

Step 1. Eligibility

Determine if the teaching is face-to-face and part of systematic instruction. Ensure the copy used is a legal copy. No restrictions on amount or type of work.

Step 2. Clarify the Exemption

Section 110(1) is for performance and display only; not for copying or distribution of a copyrighted work.

Combining a policy with a set of procedures will simplify compliance and adherence, especially if the workflow provides guidance on permissions. In my experience, the process of obtaining permission can introduce uncertainty and, because of this, many librarians, information professionals, and library users sometimes avoid or discount the process. By simply introducing or defining the terms "permission" and "licensing" and then providing a few ways to seek those out, you can take away some of the fear inherent in this aspect of the copyright system. I have also found as a copyright librarian that introducing the concept of copyright eligibility and defining it as part of a workflow or procedure can also take away some of the mystery of copyright.

Components of a Permission-to-Publish Form

Another possible procedure to include or reference in a copyright policy is an in-house permission-to-publish form. If your library has any sort of publishing program, either fee-based or free, you would want to consider having a formalized permission form tailored to your situation or institution. This is something a librarian or information professional would definitely work with a lawyer on since the document would end up becoming a formal contract. As you work with your relevant attorney on policy drafting, you could also begin conversations about drafting a content license. Attorney Richard Stim lists the following as content licensing provisions, which you could share with the library's relevant attorney as a potential starting point:[2]

- Introductory Paragraph
- The Work
- The Grant of Rights
- Sublicenses
- Reservation of Rights
- Territory
- Term
- Payments, Net Sales, Fees (if applicable)
- Warranties and Indemnity
- Copyright Registration
- Credits
- Infringement by Third Parties
- Publication Date
- Approval and Quality Control
- Licensor Copies and Right to Purchase
- Confidentiality
- Insurance
- Termination
- Dispute Resolution
- Miscellaneous Provisions

Not everything on this list will be relevant for a librarian or information professional who needs to obtain permission from a rights holder to publish a work of authorship. Knowing what elements might need to be in a content license, however, will provide you, as a librarian, with basic information on what to talk over with your library's applicable attorney.

Potential Descriptive Wording for 3-D (or Other) Printing Service Forms

The general idea behind copyright wording for a 3-D or other printing service in a library is to encourage library patrons to be cognizant of what it means to use someone else's copyrighted work. Librarians and information professionals could ask patrons for some sort of evidence of permission as a way to educate library users. Here is a brief, two-line option that could easily be added to a form:

> Users of the [3-D or other] printer warrant that they are the original creators of their prints. If using someone else's work, users need to provide evidence of permission or licensing and provide attribution to the original creator.

And here is a much longer, descriptive option suited for a website:

> Like all works covered by copyright, files for 3-D printing are protected when they are fixed in a tangible medium. The tangible medium is the .stl file. Ownership vests with the original creator of the file. The owner can determine who gets to copy, distribute, display, and adapt the contents of the file. Popular repositories like Thingiverse (https://www.thingiverse.com) get permission from the file contributor and also ask the contributor to grant a secondary license to users of the service who download files, usually one of the six licenses offered by Creative Commons. Thingiverse will include the Creative Commons license selected by the contributor on the design's webpage.
>
> The three-dimensional object that gets produced in the course of printing becomes the personal physical property of the individual making the print. No intellectual property ownership gets transferred by virtue of making the print. Users of the Do-It-Yourself 3-D printers warrant that they are the original creators of the .stl file. If using someone else's .stl file, users need to provide evidence of permission and/or licensing. If required by the license, printers need to affix the attribution label that comes with the .stl file.

Elements of an Educational or Training Program

One way to lessen the separation between a policy and daily operations is to educate and train whoever the policy's intended audience is. Designate a librarian or information professional in your organization, or perhaps volunteer yourself, to create a copyright curriculum that matches the policy and furthers the purpose of the document as well as the stated mission of the library or the institution.

Possible Training Courses to Develop

- Copyright Basics in the Digital Age for Library & Content Users
- To Portal or Publish: Managing Works of Authorship When Building a Digital Collection

- From Permission to Infringement: The Copyright Range for Educators
- Section 108: The Copyright Exemption for Librarians and Archivists

As you develop the course content, pull from the policy relevant to your library to inform details such as defining core rights, allowable exceptions and limitations, and the step-by-step procedures that help librarians, information professionals, library patrons, and content users be able to meet the policy's expectations and demands. Consider spending time training fellow librarians and information professionals on copyright terms. Defining "published," "copying," "authorship," and "tangible medium" will be useful. Rely on the terms defined earlier in this book or use the glossary available in the *Compendium*. Also consider introducing trainees to the fact that many exceptions to the core rights exist. To illustrate all these terms and concepts, a trainer can have a work of authorship in mind and use it as a hands-on demonstration.

DETERMINING A POLICY'S EFFECTIVENESS

Once a policy is in place and a set of procedures gets associated with it, consider determining its effectiveness. Evaluating a policy can take many forms from simple feedback to conducting evaluative research on efficacy.[3, 4] In formal, rigorous policy analysis, a trained analyst will look at the following areas:

- The objective, goal, or intention of the policy
- How policy maker(s) defined the problem
- The values and attitudes of the policy maker(s)
- Organizational, legal, or political concerns
- Alternative policy approaches and actionable policy recommendations[5]

One of the challenges of evaluating a copyright policy is what Stephen Gorard calls "evidence-resistant" in his book *Education Policy*, meaning it may be difficult to find evidence of the effectiveness of a copyright policy. Part of this evidence resistance stems from copyright policies often being centered on values as we have seen in the various mission statements included in chapter 3.

The foundational, value-based question that does not always explicitly get asked when defining the purpose of a policy during the drafting process is "What is copyright for?" Many librarians and information professionals will have vastly different answers to this question that might not be fully reflected in the policy either because the question was not considered during the drafting phase or because the drafters did not reflect all the possible responses in the purpose statement. This means that there are implicit values that get relayed in a policy that might not be known to those crafting the policy. Asking this question at the outset could, potentially, assist with evaluating the policy's effectiveness down the road, but it could also make moving forward with the overall policy drafting a difficult process given the range of individual attitudes and feelings librarians and information professionals have when it comes to the purpose of copyright.

Even if the values are hard to uncover, the policy, if thoroughly drafted, will, in the very least, have a purpose statement. Analyzing the effectiveness of the policy can be based on this. For example, the purpose statement of the King County Law Library Copyright Policy is "to conform with the copyright requirements for libraries under title 17 section 108 of the United States Code."[6] (Full policy available in chapter 5.) From this purpose statement, a librarian or information professional who may be analyzing the policy's effectiveness would need to determine if elements of the policy were implemented and adhered to.

Some possible investigations based on what is included in the policy would be to determine if a copyright notice is posted on copying equipment made available in the library, on computer disks that circulate, and on documents delivered through the library's interlibrary loan service. It is also important to determine that library personnel verify a copyright compliance form with the borrowing library and search for new replacement copies before copying for preservation.

Let us say in the course of analyzing the policy that it comes to light that librarians are not searching for new replacement copies before copying for preservation. The policy, in that instance, may be considered ineffective. To remedy the ineffectiveness, the applicable library manager could determine if it is an erroneous component in the policy or if it was simply a missing piece in the workflow and/or training for those involved in preservation. The library manager could quickly consult the local attorney to clarify the problem area of the policy, ensure that the policy is correct, and, if it is correct, address the matter at the workflow and training level. If, after consulting with the library's relevant attorney, it is discovered that the policy is not correct, the library administrator could work closely with the attorney and the library's governance process to update and correct the policy. Changes to procedures would also be made and any necessary training would be conducted to introduce a new process, workflow, or set of steps.

The effectiveness of some copyright policies may not be easily analyzed. For example, the policy for Somerset County Library System of New Jersey is "to support and adhere to all United States Copyright laws and regulations."[7] It is a very simple, one-line policy part of the system's overall operations manual (full document available in chapter 5). Having a single line policy may be easy in some respects, but anyone conducting a policy analysis would have to spend some time on it.

The analyst would need to ask if library personnel support the Copyright Act and also if they adhere to it. Librarians and information professionals could simply say yes to both, but what if a library employee said no? The policy could, then, potentially be less effective because of its lack of details. In what ways did the policy drafters anticipate that librarians within the library system would support the Copyright Act? And in what ways did the policy drafters expect library workers to adhere to the Copyright Act? Uncovering these details to establish effectiveness would require dedicated time and effort. If such time and effort were made possible, the information gleaned during the process could potentially be utilized to draft a more thorough policy statement, one that has a standalone purpose statement and concrete elements describing what librarians and information professionals within the library could do when copying works of authorship.

It will also be difficult, but not impossible, to analyze the policy's effectiveness in terms of patron behavior. For example, Auburn Public Library's copyright policy indicates that "library patrons may copy or print parts of copyrighted works for one-time, educational, non-profit activities. Copying that would replace or infringe [. . .] is forbidden. In such cases, library patrons should seek permission from the copyright owner before proceeding."[8] The policy also says that "library staff remind library patrons about copyright law and its restrictions, [but are not] liable for the acts of individual patrons." This element of the policy will be fairly easy to assess by simply asking library employees if this is how they interact with patrons. Assessing the policy's efficacy when it comes to patrons would be the more difficult part. The analysis would not be about whether librarians and information professionals had policed a patron's use, but whether patrons had done what the policy says, which in this instance, would be to "seek permission from the copyright owner" or copy a work only once and for non-infringing purposes. A policy analyst could ask for feedback from patrons on this topic and ensure anonymity, but this could potentially be too much and frighten away patrons or alienate them. Another, less direct approach could be to incorporate the policy requirement into appropriate service areas, such as asking for evidence of permission when a patron uses a library's 3-D printing service, as mentioned earlier in this chapter.

The goal in assessing effectiveness will be to match the inquiry to the purpose statement. For example, the purpose of Louisville Catholic Schools' copyright policy is to ensure that "the workman shall receive just compensation for his labor."[9] The analysis of the policy's effectiveness could include determining if librarians and teachers relied more on direct purchase of material instead of the various exceptions allowed for in making copies of works of authorship. The larger policy document (available in chapter 5) also incorporates guidelines for teachers about how much they can copy, which a policy analyst could look at and ask teachers how much they adhere to the guidelines. These conversations, overall, could potentially lead to a slightly altered purpose statement that reflects both the "just compensation" aspect as well as the fair use principles that are clearly valued by teachers at Louisville Catholic Schools.

Assessing policy effectiveness at a large institution or at a library that serves a populous area will be equally difficult, but, again, not impossible. For example, the purpose of the University of Utah's copyright policy is to ensure compliance. The general principles state that employees "are expected to recognize and observe the exclusive rights of copyright owners."[10] An analysis of the policy's effectiveness would need to evaluate the degree to which the institution's 20,000+ employees know and understand the exclusive rights. It is possible that a brief survey could be conducted to uncover this information for purposes of determining the policy's effectiveness. The general principles also state that the policy's purpose is to "promote and facilitate academic uses of copyrighted materials and to reduce incidences of copyright infringement." Analyzing these aspects of the policy could utilize an audit of academic uses of copyrighted materials and/or determine if the institution has received any infringement complaints. These sources of evidence could potentially help assess the policy's effectiveness.

The degree to which workflows and training documents are tied to a policy document could serve as an additional mechanism for analyzing a policy's efficacy. Policy drafters could consider including a section dedicated to procedures and include workflow documentation within that section. The level to which the procedures get adopted might not completely inform the question of effectiveness, but it can serve as a somewhat reliable element within the overall process.

In conclusion, this chapter has demonstrated that policies are complex documents that incorporate both values and expectations of behavior. It can be challenging to remain value-neutral when drafting policies and equally challenging to unpack those values and expectations in the process of analyzing a policy's effectiveness. It can also be challenging to figure out ways to translate the values and behavior expectations into day-to-day library operations. To that end, this chapter explored ways of incorporating a policy into the daily work of librarians and information professionals. Potential copyright-related workflows were included as well as possible forms and educational training options. This chapter also discussed ways of analyzing a policy's effectiveness as a means for uncovering and coming to know the purpose and intent of a policy. This type of analysis, while potentially difficult and time-consuming work, can assist in ensuring transparency and efficiency.

In the next chapter, example policies in their entirety are included in order to provide readers with greater guidance.

NOTES

1. U.S. Copyright Office. *Section 110(1)*. Accessed August 2, 2019. https://www.copyright.gov/title17/92chap1.html#110.

2. Stim, Richard. *Content License Provisions: The Basics*, a paper handout provided at the 32nd Annual Meeting of the Society for Scholarly Publishing. San Francisco, CA: Society for Scholarly Publishing Meeting, June 2, 2010.

3. Landry, Larry. *City Council Members: Issues in Policy Effectiveness*. Tempe, Arizona: Center for Public Affairs, 1977.

4. Sgherri, Silvia; Bayoumi, Tamim. *On Impatience and Policy Effectiveness*. Washington, DC: International Monetary Fund, 2009.

5. Friedman, Lee S. *Does Policy Analysis Matter? Exploring Its Effectiveness in Theory and Practice*. Oakland, CA: University of California Press, 2016.

6. King County Law Library. *King County Law Library Copyright Policy & Intellectual Property Statement.* Accessed July 26, 2019. http://kcll.org/contact-us/policies/copyright-policy-intellectual-property-statement/.

7. Somerset County Library System of New Jersey. *Somerset County Library System—Policy Manual.* Accessed July 26, 2019. https://s40873y1pyb1ozqsg275 sisu-wpengine.netdna-ssl.com/wp-content/uploads/M-Collection-Management -Policy.pdf.

8. Auburn Public Library. *Copyright.* Accessed July 26, 2019. http://www .auburnpubliclibrary.org/about-the-library/apl-policies/copyright/.

9. Louisville Catholic Schools. *Library Media Guidelines.* Accessed July 26, 2019. http://louisvillecatholicschools.com/wp-content/uploads/2017/01/ LibraryMediaGuidelines.pdf.

10. University of Utah. *Copyright Policy: Copying of Copyrighted Works.* Accessed July 26, 2019. https://regulations.utah.edu/research/7-013.php.

Sample Policies

This chapter offers sample policies for librarians and information professionals to utilize as examples and models. Some of the policies have been mentioned already throughout the previous chapters, but they are included here in their entirety for ease of reference. The policies are included by permission, and each document includes a brief paragraph describing the strong elements of each document. The chapter includes three samples from libraries within educational institutions, four from libraries part of government or public entities, and one from a library part of a private, nonprofit society. Sample policies from corporate libraries could not be located.

The main components to look for as you read through the sample policies include the type of policy and definition of terms. Once you have a good idea of the kind of copyright policy that is in front of you, you will be able to quickly pull out elements that will support you in either revising an existing policy or developing a new one. Each of these example documents treat the copyright exemptions discussed throughout this book in various ways, but most of them highlight Section 107 Fair Use. Most of the sample policies apply to either teachers or library employees, but some provide guidance to library users. Auburn Public Library's policy does this as does the LifeDiscoveryEd Digital Library.

King County Law Library focuses only on Section 108 Libraries & Archives. The National Park Service provides guidance to employees about showing movies or playing music. Snow College Libraries incorporates Section 110(1) Face-to-Face Teaching in order to address the question of showing copyrighted movies in the library. The LifeDiscoveryEd Digital Library's policy includes instructions about obtaining permission to publish and also utilizes its policy to grant permission for library patrons to reuse their copyrighted content by means of Creative Commons licensing.

LIBRARIES WITHIN EDUCATIONAL INSTITUTIONS

Louisville Catholic Schools

The policy at Louisville Catholic Schools is thorough and robust. It includes the institution's mission and value statement alongside the policy. The policy places an emphasis on Section 107 Fair Use. It could also consider including Section 108 Libraries & Archives and Section 110(1) Face-to-Face Teaching. See figure 5.1.

LIBRARY MEDIA GUIDELINES

Table of Contents

FIGURE 5.1

Library Media Guidelines. *Louisville Catholic Schools, http://louisvillecatholicschools .com/wp-content/uploads/2017/01/LibraryMediaGuidelines.pdf.*

LIBRARY MEDIA CENTER GOALS

In accordance with the <u>Archdiocese of Louisville Handbook</u>, schools should adopt the following goals for its library media center:

1. To provide a well-developed and well-maintained library in the school. The library facility serves primarily as the center for educational research and as a resource for teachers, students, and parents in achieving curriculum outcomes.

2. To provide books and media materials to support the instructional program. All materials will be
   a. consistent with the mission of the Catholic school
   b. supportive of the religious formation and intellectual, ethical, cultural, and social development of the student
   c. designed to give access to ideas essential to the development of students' critical thinking skills and decision-making processes.

3. To keep an up-to-date inventory of all library materials and audio-visual equipment with records of the circulation and location of media materials preferably using an automated catalog and circulation system.

4. To provide access to CD ROM and Internet technology, as well as current print reference and periodical resources, for the purpose of research.

COPYRIGHT POLICY

CHRISTIAN VALUE: Christ taught that the workman shall receive just compensation for his labor. In following this teaching:

"Copyright is a form of protection provided by the laws of the United States (title 17, U. S. Code) to the authors of "original works of authorship," including literary, dramatic, musical, artistic, and certain other intellectual works. It is illegal for anyone to violate any of the rights provided by the copyright law to the owner of copyright. These rights, however, are not unlimited in scope. Sections 107 through 121 of the 1976 Copyright Act establish limitations on these rights. One major limitation is the doctrine of "fair use," which is given a statutory basis in section 107 of the 1976 Copyright Act." [1]

Regulations: Guidelines to schools will be provided from the Office of Lifelong Formation and Education and will be updated as needed to reflect both changes in federal and state laws and changes in media production techniques.

---

[1] <u>Copyright Basics</u>. U.S. Copyright Office. July 2008. 22 July 2009. <http://www.copyright.gov/circs/circ1.pdf>.

FIGURE 5.1
(continued)

FAIR USE PRINCIPLES

The National Council of Teachers of English has identified five principles of fair use for media literacy.

Principle One: Under fair use, educators using the concept and techniques of media literacy can choose illustrative material from the full range of copyrighted sources and make them available to learners, in class, in workshops, in informal mentoring and teaching settings, and on school-related Web sites.

Educators may use any media to achieve their lesson goal or purpose. They should use only what is necessary to illustrate their purpose, which could be a short excerpt or the whole work and should use proper citation.

Principle Two: Under fair use, educators using the concepts and techniques of media literacy can integrate copyrighted material into the curriculum materials, including books, workbooks, podcasts, DVD compilations, video, Web sites, and other materials designed for learning.

Educators should use only what is needed to reach their goal, use proper citation, and the media should meet professional standards.

Principle Three: Educators using concepts and techniques of media literacy should be able to share effective examples of teaching about media and meaning with one another, including lessons and resource materials. If curriculum developers are making sound decisions on fair use when they create their materials, then their work should be able to be seen, used, and even purchased by anyone—since fair use applies to commercial materials as well as those produced outside the marketplace model.

Educators should use care when using portions of copyrighted materials to share professionally, using only what is necessary to illustrate the educational objectives of the lesson. For promoting purposes permission or a license should be obtained.

Principle Four: Because media literacy education cannot thrive unless learners themselves have the opportunity to learn about how media functions at the most practical level, educators using concepts and techniques of media literacy should be free to enable learners to incorporate, modify, and re-present existing media objects in their own classroom work. Media production can foster and deepen awareness of the constructed nature of all media, one of the key concepts of media literacy. The basis for fair use here is embedded in good pedagogy.

Students may use copyrighted material but should not substitute it for their own creative work. For example students may use copyrighted music in their projects but it must have an educational purpose and should not be used for its popularity. Also proper citation should be given.

Principle Five: Educators should work with learners to make a reasoned decision about distribution that reflects sound pedagogy and ethical values. In some cases, widespread distribution of students' work (via the Internet, for example) is appropriate. If student work that incorporates, modifies, and re-presents existing media content meets the transformativeness standard, it can be distributed to wide audiences under the doctrine of fair use.

Educators should instruct students to behave responsibly when using copyrighted materials within their classroom projects. Student work that is distributed for school wide events or conferences should meet fair use policy.

FIGURE 5.1
(continued)

COPYRIGHT GUIDELINES

Television/VHS/DVD Programs

Kentucky Educational Television (KET) programs provided for use in the schools of the Archdiocese of Louisville have more liberal school off-air recording and use rights than any other source of video programming. The annual KET Schedule Book clearly states the right of each of these programs.

All other video programs, from commercial TV, cable TV, public TV, video stores and other sources of video programs, carry special, individual restrictions. Many absolutely prohibit recording and use, even in schools.

Equipment from schools in the Archdiocese of Louisville must not be used for making illegal copies. In order to adhere to copyright laws, it is deemed essential that employees of the school abide by the following regulations:

1. Videotape usage (off-air recording, rental or purchase) requires completion of the appropriate forms prior to taping and playback)

2. A rented or purchased videotape may be used in the school only for curriculum related instruction by an individual teacher, not for entertainment or reward, unless a public performance license has been obtained.

3. The presentation must use a legitimate copy of the videotape, and attendance must be limited to the teacher and pupils. The performance must be part of the teaching activities of a nonprofit institution, and it must take place in a classroom or similar place devoted to instruction.

4. Off-air recordings within schools are permissible only at the written request of an individual teacher for classroom instructional purposes, and may not be regularly recorded in anticipation of requests. The tape cannot be used by other teachers. This applies only to those programs that are provided to the general public at no charge.

5. Off-air recordings may be used once by individual teachers in the course of relevant teaching activities, and repeated once only when instructional reinforcement is necessary, in classrooms and similar places devoted to instruction within a single building, cluster or campus, as well as in the homes of students receiving formalized home instruction, during the first ten (10) consecutive school days in the forty-five (45) calendar day retention period. "School days" are school session days – not counting holidays, vacations, examination periods, or other scheduled interruptions-within forty-five (45) calendar day retention period.

6. A limited number of copies may be reproduced from each off-air recording to meet the legitimate needs of teachers under these guidelines. Each such additional copy shall be subject to all provisions governing the original recording.

7. Off-air recordings need not be used in there entirely, but the recorded programs may not be altered from their original content. Off-air recordings may not be physically or electronically combined or merged to constitute teaching anthologies or compilations.

8. All copies of off-air recordings must include the copyright notice on the broadcast program as recorded.

9. Educational institutions are expected to establish appropriate control procedures to maintain the integrity of these guidelines.

10. Recordings of Television/VHS/DVD programs may not be transferred to other formats.

FIGURE 5.1
(continued)

COPYRIGHT GUIDELINES

Computer Software

1. Equipment from the school must not be used for making illegal copies of software.

2. The use of illegally copied software in schools or offices is prohibited.

3. Software licensing agreements of copyright holders must be observed.

4. Multiple loading of software is prohibited unless written permission has been obtained.

5. Use of computer software on a network computer system is prohibited unless written permission is obtained.

6. All software obtained from district site licensing is for classroom/office use only, unless written permission has been obtained.

Print/Graphics

1. The reproduction of copyrighted, consumable materials such as workbooks, activity sheet, etc., is specifically prohibited by the copyright law.

2. One copy only may be made for a transparency for classroom instructional use.

3. Teachers or students may not make multiple copies of copyrighted materials from a library or other reference including out-of print texts.

4. Copying from printed publications such as a poem, a chapter from a book, and/or a short article from a periodical are limited to a single copy for research use.

5. Any copyrighted syndicated comic strip or cartoon character may not be reproduced or altered for bulletin boards, hallways, or walls without written permission.

Music

1. Music recording may not be reproduced from one medium to another (e.g. Cassette to CD).

2. Music for use as background music of a slide presentation is permitted only if the presentation is required for instructional purposes, and not entertainment.

3. Sheet music may not be copied unless the music is on order and has not yet been received by the teacher. An order must have been placed. Any copies must be destroyed once the purchased materials are received.

4. Recordings of music may not be transferred from an audio broadcast to tape.

FIGURE 5.1
(continued)

COPYRIGHT--TEACHER FACT SHEET[2]

Books

PERMITTED
- single copy: chapter of book
- single copy: article from magazine or newspaper
- single copy: short story, short essay, short poem
- single copy: chart, graph, diagram, picture or non
- syndicated, non-copyrighted cartoon

NOT PERMITTED
- copying several chapters per book
- copying several articles per magazine
- copying consumables: workbooks, copyrighted
- exercise sheets, tests
- photocopying worn dittomasters

Multiple copies for classroom/instructional purposes

PERMITTED
- complete poem less than 250 words (not more than 2 pages)
- excerpt from long poem not to exceed 250 words
- article, story, or essay less than 2,500 words
- excerpt (from above) less than 1,000 words or 10% of total, whichever is less
- one chart, graph, diagram, picture, or non-syndicated, non-copyrighted cartoon per book or periodical
- works combining prose, poetry, etc., less than 10% of whole
- IF.....
    - copying is for one course only
    - insufficient time to request permission
    - one work from a single author
    - less than 3 authors from collective work
    - 9 or less instances of multiple copying per term
    - copying not used to create or replace anthologies
    - same copying not repeated next term
    - students not charged beyond photocopying fees
- classroom quantities of current news articles if individual articles not copyrighted
- All multiple copying must be at the inspiration of the individual teacher and the decision to use the material so close to the date needed for instruction as to preclude securing copyright permission from the copyright holder

NOT PERMITTED
- using/making multiple copies of same material semester after semester
- creating "anthologies"
- copying workbooks and other works meant to be used once by one student
- copying shall not be directed by higher authority
- copying more than one or two excerpts from a single author during one class term
- copying from workbooks, tests, or other consumables. copying a blacklined master.

Big Books

PERMITTED
- one illustration per book
- two pages per book as long as they don't comprise more than 10% of the book
- **Note**: Occasionally publishers of big books have given the District permission to copy that exceeds the normal fair use guidelines. Any letters granting additional permission will be kept on file in library.

NOT PERMITTED
- copying "just" the text from a big book or picture book
- making an audio-tape of someone narrating a big book or picture book

[2] "Copyright Guidelines." JeffCo Public Schools. Jefferson County Public Schools. Golden, CO. 22 July 2009. < http://jeffcoweb.jeffco.k12.co.us/isu/library/copyright.html>.

FIGURE 5.1
(continued)

Audiovisual Materials

PERMITTED
- creating slide sets from books, magazines, etc., as long as only one per source used
- making one overhead transparency of one page of one workbook
- converting a damaged filmstrip to a slide set, keeping same order minus damaged frames
- enlarging a map with an opaque projector for tracing but not duplicating color scheme, symbols, etc.
- copying non-dramatic literary, audiovisual works for use by blind or deaf individuals

NOT PERMITTED
- copying audio tapes or video tapes for archival or backup purposes
- reproducing musical works or converting from one form to another (record to cassette)
- copying any audiovisual work in its entirety (except off-air taping)
- converting from one medium format to another
- recording the text of a book or textbook onto an audiocassette

Music

PERMITTED
- emergency copies for performance provided copies are later purchased
- for study or teaching, single or multiple copies of excerpts
- IF.....
  - o excerpts do not constitute a performable unit such as a movement or aria
- editing purchased copies for simplification
- IF.....
  - o character of work is not changed
  - o lyrics are not changed
- single copy of performances by students made for evaluation or rehearsal purposes
- copy of recording for purposes of aural testing
- portion of commercial music played as background in student media production

NOT PERMITTED
- copying for performances
- copying to create anthologies
- copying to avoid purchasing
- copying but excluding copyright notice
- performing a work without a license or paying royalty fees

Video (Educational/Instructional OFF-AIR Taping)

PERMITTED
- may record program OFF-AIR
- IF.....
  - o program is used for instructional purposes, or face-to-face teaching, not for entertainment or filler
  - o program is requested by a teacher
  - o program is shown once and repeated once per class by individual teacher during first 10 consecutive school days after broadcast
  - o program is not retained beyond 45 calendar days
  - o program is recorded in its entirety (need not be used in its entirety)
  - o after first 10 consecutive school days, program is used only for evaluation by teacher

NOT PERMITTED
- videotaping in anticipation of requests
- retaining a program longer than 45 days
- showing a program after ten days
- showing for motivation, filler, or entertainment purposes
- taping a program at home, using in the classroom, and subsequently retaining in personal collection

FIGURE 5.1
(continued)

Video (OFF-AIR Taping at Home)

PERMITTED
- may tape program at home and bring to school to use but all educational guidelines must be followed
- may show "home" tape if above criteria are followed and if tape legally made

NOT PERMITTED
- individual who taped program may not retain it

Video (Cable)

PERMITTED
- may tape programs being simultaneously broadcast (see OFF-AIR educational/ instructional guidelines)
- may show videos or motion pictures via cable within a building as long as programs are used in face-to-face teaching and are of an instructional nature

NOT PERMITTED
- may not tape programs not being broadcast simultaneously (CNN, Discovery, Disney, HBO, etc.) unless prior approval or license obtained from cable network
- may not show programs of a musical, dramatic, or entertainment nature
- may not copy cable or satellite programs without permission. Note: Educators may use cable magazines, like Cable in the Classroom for varying copying/retention rights of individual programs.

Video (purchased or rented)

PERMITTED
- showing purchased or rented videotape for curriculum-supported, face-to-face teaching activities

NOT PERMITTED
- showing purchased or rented videotape for entertainment, rewards, rainy days, filler, or non-instructional purposes.
- **Note:** Performance rights may be acquired at time of purchase; then it's legal to show such videos for non-instructional events.

Video (Satellite Transmissions)

PERMITTED
- copying from a satellite transmission will depend on the contractual agreement with the satellite company.

NOT PERMITTED
- copies of motion pictures, other AV works, choreographic works and pantomimes
- copies of broadcasts that are of a "general cultural nature" or intended for transmission as part of an information storage and retrieval system

Software

PERMITTED
- copying into RAM if copying is necessary to use the program
- one copy for archival purposes
- probably may make a 3.5" disk from a 5 1/4" disk if the 5 1/4" disk is considered the archival copy
- back up copies of hard drives as long as they are not used to run another drive
- library lending of public domain software

NOT PERMITTED
- circulation of archival copy
- "networking" software without license or permission
- loading a single copy of a software program onto several computers for simultaneous use
- making copies of copyrighted software for student use

FIGURE 5.1
(continued)

Databases

PERMITTED
- may download searches

NOT PERMITTED
- downloaded searches should not be retained
- downloaded material may not be used to create a derivative work

CD-ROM

PERMITTED
- printing out pages of reference or other works for study or teaching

NOT PERMITTED
- printing out large section of work

Musicals, Dramatic, and Non-Dramatic Performances

PERMITTED
- school chorus performance open to the public

NOT PERMITTED
- school drama club performing copyrighted play broadcast over cable to classes
- recording of choral or instrumental concerts and then giving or selling recording to parents

Multimedia

PERMITTED
- teacher or student-developed multimedia program of copyrighted programs for use in classroom only
- **Note:** Students may keep their work indefinitely; teachers may keep their work for only two years.
- IF: the following limitations are observed:
  - Motion media
    - use of up to 10% or 3 min., whichever is less, of an individual program
  - Text
    - up to 10% or 1000 words, whichever is less; short poems less than 250 words may be used in their entirety;
  - Music
    - Up to 10% but no more than 30 sec. From a single work (or combined from separate extracts of a work);
  - Illustrations, cartoons, photographs
    - no more than 5 images from a single artist or photographer, no more than 10% or 15 images from a single collective work;
  - Numerical data sets
    - up to 10% or 2,550 fields or cells whichever is less

NOT PERMITTED
- teacher or student-developed multimedia program of copyrighted works for use in displays, festivals, parent meetings or other public events

FIGURE 5.1
(continued)

Internet

PERMITTED
- downloading public domain software

NOT PERMITTED
- uploading copyrighted software to Internet for downloading
- collecting materials off the Internet and compiling into a new work
- forwarding material off the Internet to friends, co-workers

Digital

PERMITTED

NOT PERMITTED
- digitizing a copyrighted slide collection
- scanning copyrighted materials (magazine photograph, cartoon illustration, etc.) for school newspaper

Graphics

PERMITTED
- one graphic per book or periodical;
- multiple copies of a single graphic
- **IF...**
  - copying is at the instance/inspiration of teacher; copy is for only one course in the school;
  - here are not more than nine occurrences of multiple copying for that course; and not more than one graphic is copied per book or periodical.

NOT PERMITTED
- adaptation of a popular cartoon character for the school mascot;
- copying an image from a coloring book for a worksheet;
- making stuffed animals of popular picture book characters;
- scanning a cartoon into school newsletter;

FIGURE 5.1
(continued)

VIDEO RECORDING PLAYBACK REQUEST AND STATEMENT POLICY

I hereby request that the following video program be played for my class use and/or evaluation.

Name of Program to be telecast _____

Date of Telecast _____ In-house Channel # _____ or _____ Classroom VCR/DVD

Length of Telecast _____

This program is applicable to the following Course of Study:

GUIDELINES FOR THE PLAYBACK OF ANY VIDEO IN ANY SCHOOL LOCATION

1. The videotape is either a legally copyrighted copy and/or meets off-air videotape guidelines.

2. Playback of the requested video recording is in the course of a relevant teaching activity.

3. Even though this recording may not be used in its entirety, the recording shall not be altered form its original content.

These guidelines apply to all video recordings used in all school locations.

I, the undersigned, have read and understand that written above; I furthermore, agree to abide by the Fair Use Doctrine as applies to the 1978 Copyright Act.

Signature_____ Date_____

REMEMBER: SCHOOL EQUIPMENT CANNOT BE USED TO DUPLICATE OR RUN ILLEGAL MATERIAL.

This paper is to be retained in school files.

FIGURE 5.1
(continued)

COLLECTION DEVELOPMENT: SELECTION

The primary objective of the Catholic School Library Media Center is to support and enrich the school and its curriculum. It is the obligation of the Catholic School Library Media Center to provide materials which are consistent with the mission of the Catholic school and which give access to ideas essential to the student's development of skills needed for critical thinking and responsible decision making.

The materials selected will be:
1. Consistent with the mission of the Catholic School.
2. Supportive of the religious formation and intellectual, ethical, cultural and social development of the student.

CRITERIA FOR SELECTION: Selected materials shall conform to the following criteria as they apply:

1. Materials shall support and be consistent with Archdiocesan goals and curricular objectives as described in the Archdiocese Handbook for Catholic Schools.

2. Materials should be interesting, accurate, stimulating and significant in content. Materials should have format and style of high quality and be appropriate to the expression of the idea of the material. Technical production should be of high quality and appropriate to the medium.

3. The concepts presented should be within the understanding of the students who will use the materials and provide for a diversity of interests and levels of ability.

4. Materials concerned with racial, religious, sexual, or ethnic differences shall be free from stereotype, caricature, and other characteristics likely to misrepresent, offend, or defame particular segments of society.

5. Materials should contribute to lifelong learning by widening boundaries of thought, presenting a realistic picture of life, developing an understanding and respect of people and their values, and fostering positive values.

6. Materials should justify the cost in relation to anticipated use. When materials become outdated by newer information and technology, replacement costs should be considered.

PROCEDURES FOR SELECTION:

1. The Library Media Specialist will evaluate the Library Media Center's existing materials collection and curriculum needs and by consulting reputable, professional aids and other appropriate sources, select materials that will support the curriculum objectives of the school. Examples of professional resources would include, but not be limited to:
   Booklist
   Elementary School Library Collection
   Horn Book
   Kirkus Reviews
   School Library Journal
   Other bibliographies

2. Selection recommendations will be sought from teachers and students as appropriate.

3. Gifts and donations to the Library Media Center shall be reviewed using the same selection criteria and accepted or rejected accordingly.

FIGURE 5.1
(continued)

COLLECTION DEVELOPMENT: INVENTORY

The Library Media Specialist should conduct a full inventory or partial inventory spread over time to:
- Account for each item (database)
- Note discrepancies between records and materials
- Replacement/weeding policies as discrepancies are noted

The inventory allows the LMS to check the currency and the condition of the available resources as well as determine which resources are missing from the collection. The inventory also indicates which resources should be discarded due to age or irrelevance to the curriculum. After reviewing the inventory results the LMS can prioritize future purchases and possibly identify curricular areas to be supplemented by online resources. In addition, the inventory ensures that all resources are located in the proper location on the shelves for easier access at the beginning of the school year."

According to the Alpine School District in Utah's "Guidelines for Media Center Management: Collection Inventory," the purpose of doing inventory work, though time consuming, is critical to good management and operations of any school media center or any other library. The following information is directly from these guidelines.

BOOK INVENTORY

An accurate book collection inventory can help a media specialist in many ways:

1. It identifies missing items. These can then be replaced if that is appropriate.

2. It can help you discover items that may be cataloged improperly for your collection. As you take regular inventories of your book collection, items that are incorrectly cataloged should catch your eye.

3. It helps identify items that should be removed from circulation, or weeded.

4. It helps you detect items that need repairing. However, the process of doing an inventory will only reveal obvious needs. Make sure you also use other methods, such as checking books for needed repairs when they are checked in during circulation.

5. It helps you locate "lost in-house" (incorrectly shelved) items. The process of "reading shelves" should not be overlooked in lieu of a yearly inventory. [3]

ELECTRONIC INVENTORY

All automated software has an inventory function as part of the program. The LMS will use a handheld scanner to gather data for the inventory reports. This is preferred; however, if it is not available, inventory may be conducted using an up-to-date shelf list.

---

[3] "Guidelines for Media Center Management: Collection Inventory." Alpine School District. 22 July 2009.
<http://www.alpine.k12.ut.us/depts/media/elemlessons_rev/m6-mc_management/lesson4inventory.html >.

FIGURE 5.1
(continued)

COLLECTION DEVELOPMENT: EVALUATION

The Archdiocese of Louisville promotes the CREW Method (Continuous Review, Evaluation, and Weeding) for all LMCs.

CREW Formula = i.e. 5/3 MUSTIE = 5 years from copyright, 3 years since last circulation, various factors

OVERVIEW CHART OF CREW FORMULAS

Dewey Class

000	004	3/X/MUSTIE
	011	10/X/MUSTIE
	020	10/3/MUSTIE
	030	5/X/MUSTIE
	Others	5/X/MUSTIE
100	133	15/3/MUSTIE
	150	10/3/MUSTIE
	160	10/3/MUSTIE
200		10/3/MUSTIE or
		5/3/MUSTIE
300	310	2/X/MUSTIE
	320	5/3/MUSTIE
		(Topical)
		10/3/MUSTIE
		(Historical)
	330	5/3/MUSTIE
	340	10/X/MUSTIE
	350	10/X/MUSTIE
	360	5/X/MUSTIE
	370	10/3/MUSTIE
	390	5/3/MUSTIE
		(Etiquette)
		10/3/MUSTIE
		(Folklore/Customs)
400		10/3/MUSTIE
500	510	10/3/MUSTIE
	550	X/3/MUSTIE
	570	10/3/MUSTIE
	580	10/3/MUSTIE
600	610	5/3/MUSTIE
	630	5 /3/MUSTIE
	635	10/3/MUSTIE
	640	5/3/MUSTIE
	649	5/3/MUSTIE
	690	10/3/MUSTIE
	Others	5/3/MUSTIE

FIGURE 5.1
(continued)

700	745	X/3/MUSTIE
	770	5/3/MUSTIE
	790	10/3/MUSTIE
	Others	X/X/MUSTIE
800		X/X/MUSTIE
900	910	5/3/MUSTIE
		(Geography and Guide Books)
		10/3/MUSTIE
		(Personal Narratives)
	Others	15/3/MUSTIE
B (Biography)		X/2/MUSTIE
F (Fiction)		X/2/MUSTIE
E (Easy Picture Books)		X/2/MUSTIE
Periodicals/Newspapers		3/X/X
AV		2/X/WORST
Donations		X/X/MUSTIE

MUSTIE is an easily remembered acronym for six negative factors that frequently ruin a book's usefulness and mark it for weeding:

M = **M**isleading (and/or factually inaccurate)
U = **U**gly (worn and beyond mending or rebinding)
S = **S**uperseded (by a truly new edition or by a much better book on the subject)
T = **T**rivial (of no discernible literary or scientific merit)
I = **I**rrelevant to the needs and interests of your community
E = The material may be obtained expeditiously **E**lsewhere through interlibrary loan or reciprocal borrowing.[4]

Audiovisual materials use the acronym WORST.
W = **W**orn out
O = **O**ut of date
R = **R**arely used
S = **S**ystem headquarters can supply
T = **T**rivial and faddish
Since many media are costly, weeding of such materials, once acquired, must be done as carefully and cautiously as the initial selection of acquisition.

[4] Larson, Jeanette. The CREW method : expanded guidelines for collection evaluation and weeding for small and medium-sized public libraries. Austin, Tex. : Texas State Library, 2008. 22 July 2009. <http://www.tsl.state.tx.us/ld/pubs/crew/index.html>.

FIGURE 5.1
(continued)

COLLECTION DEVELOPMENT: DESELECTION

Every school will follow approved criteria and procedures to remove from the library materials that have out-lived their usefulness to the instructional program. The Library Media specialist will establish an ongoing procedure for removal of materials which become outdated, worn, or no longer appropriate.

CRITERIA FOR DESELCTION

A small, attractive, and up to date collection, relevant to the curriculum, is of greater use to students and faculty than a large storehouse of unused material. The American Library Association has identified the following criteria for deselection (weeding):

1. To utilize most economically the available space in the library, use community resources such as the Public Library for material that is seldom used in the collection.
2. To give the library a reputation for reliability.
3. To remove the illusion of a well-stocked library, which would discourage needed increases in the library media budget.
4. To increase circulation by removing unattractive material and spotlighting the remaining materials.
5. To identify areas of strength and weakness of the collection; to identify materials needing repair.[5]

Deselection should be done on a regular, continuous basis. Quantity is not the objective of the library collection. The goal is not to have a great abundance of books, but rather to have the right books for the right students at the right time.

CRITERIA FOR DISCARDING MATERIALS

1. Poor physical shape
   a. Film or paper brittle
   b. Color faded
   c. Paper yellowed or torn
   d. Discs or book covers scratched or warped
   e. Bindings ragged
   f. Obsolete
2. Poor format
   a. Small print
   b. Poor quality pictures.
3. Poor content
   a. Discriminatory
   b. Out of date, especially computers, science, medicine, health, technology, geography, travel, transportation careers
   c. Trivial subject or approach
   d. Mediocre writing
   e. Inaccurate or false information
   f. Repetitious series
   g. Superseded editions
   h. Not on standard lists
   i. Not defended by subject specialist or teacher
4. Inappropriate for the specific collection
   a. Neither circulated nor used for reference
   b. Unneeded duplicates
   c. Unneeded titles in little-used subject areas. Retain a few basic titles
   d. Interest or reading level inappropriate for students
   e. Change in curriculum and/or age group served
5. What not to weed
   a. Classics, except when more attractive format is available
   b. Local and Kentucky history, unless can be replaced with new copies
   c. Annuals and other major publications of the school or community college
   d. Materials, which could be considered archival, if no other unit of the institution, maintain such files
   e. Items incorrectly classified or poorly promoted which might circulate under changed circumstances

---

[5] Segal, Joseph P. Evaluating and Weeding Collections in Small and Medium Sized Libraries. Chicago: American Library Association. 1980.

FIGURE 5.1
(continued)

COLLECTION DEVELOPMENT: SHELF LIFE OF PRINT AND NONPRINT MATERIAL

Information becomes out-dated. In general, material becomes out-dated as follows:

In one year:
> Replace each year with most recent publication
>> Almanacs
>> Yearbooks
>> Statistical Publications
>> Unindexed periodicals

In Three Years:
> Technology materials (especially materials describing newest equipment)

In Five Years:
> Pure Science (Dewey 500's) Examine for currency, except for Botany and Natural History
> Careers
> General Encyclopedias
> Atlases and globes

In Five to Ten Years:
> Geography

Between Ten and Twenty Years:
> Bibliographies – You may want to keep in Librarian's office for personal reference
> Dictionaries
> Biographies – Once well-known people need to be replaced by living personalities
>> Or persons related to curriculum
> Craft books
> Personal health and hygiene
> Sports books –Watch for changes in the rules and personalities associated with the sport.
>> Weed out sexist material.

Over Twenty Years:
> Single volume reference books such as reference books such as, Facts about Presidents, Bartlett's' Familiar Quotations, Webster's Biographical Dictionary, and Webster's Geographical Dictionary
> Craft books[6]

---

[6] Slote, Stanley J. Weeding Library Collections II. 2nd rev. ed. Littleton, CO: Libraries Unlimited, Inc., 1982.

FIGURE 5.1
(continued)

COLLECTION DEVELOPMENT: DISPOSAL OF OBSOLETE MATERIALS

If a book purchased with Title Funds has been weeded from the school collection, the librarian must do several things for proper disposal. First, the title page must be torn out. After all title pages have been torn out, a list of books by author and the title pages should be sent to the Title VI office at the county board of education. In Jefferson County the contact is currently (2009) Kelly Hoover. She can be reached at 502-485-3288. Schools in other counties should consult their LEA for specific instructions. The books themselves may be discarded.

If equipment purchased with title funds is determined to be obsolete, the LEA should be contacted to pick up the equipment. In Jefferson County the contact is currently (2009) Kelly Hoover. She can be reached at 502-485-3288. Schools in other counties should consult their LEA for specific instructions.

All equipment and books purchased with non-title funds may be disposed of at the discretion of the library media specialist in compliance with local school guidelines.

FIGURE 5.1
(continued)

RECONSIDERATION

Despite the quality of the selection process, occasional objections to library media materials will be made. Catholic Schools support the church's respect for intellectual inquiry as well as the principals of intellectual freedom expressed in the First Amendment of the Constitution of the United States, the Library Bill of Rights of the American Library Association, and the Students' Right to Read of the National Council of Teachers of English.

When materials are questioned, the policy should be to balance the principles of intellectual inquiry expressed in these documents, the right of the student to access information and the integrity of the school as part of the Catholic community.

The process for requesting review and re-evaluation of materials functions at all levels in the Archdiocese. In schools without a library media specialist, the library aide will act at the direction of the principal to respond to requests for review and re-evaluation.

PROCEDURE FOR RECONSIDERATION (Local)

1. When a request is made about library material, the library media specialist will ask the person/group to complete a reconsideration form.
2. The reconsideration form will be sent by the concerned party to the principal.
3. The principal shall forward the original or copy of the request to the library media specialist within one day of receiving it.
4. The library media specialist and the principal will review the request and will together try to resolve the request within 10 working days.
5. If the request is not resolved by the principal and library media specialist within this timeframe, a reconsideration committee can be convened. This reconsideration committee will be made up of no more than nine members of the local School Board. It may include the library media specialist, a reading teacher, and/or levels coordinator, religious education teacher, parent, teacher representative, or other representatives as designated by the School Board. The materials will not be removed from circulation until a decision is made.
6. The reconsideration committee will meet within fifteen days of the request. At that time the committee will hear the request and examine the material. A decision of the reconsideration committee will be made within ten working days following this meeting.
7. The reconsideration committee can make the following recommendations to the school principal and the school board.
   a. To take no action to remove the material. (Deny the request.)
   b. To remove all or part of the challenged material.
   c. To limit the use of the challenged material.

PROCEDURE FOR RECONSIDERATION (Archdiocesan)

If the concerned party wishes to challenge the decision of the reconsideration committee, the process begins again at the diocesan level.

1. When a request is referred to the Archdiocese, the Consultant and the Superintendent will work together to try to resolve the request. If the request is not resolved within five working days from the date of the referral to the Archdiocese, the material will be given to a reconsideration committee.
2. The reconsideration committee at the archdiocesan level will consist of no more that nine members. Members may include library media specialists from other Catholic schools, members of the Academy of Catholic Educators, a theologian/religious education expert, and other persons designated by the Superintendent.
3. The reconsideration committee will meet within fifteen working days. At that time the reconsideration committee will hear the request, examine the material, and examine the decision of the local school reconsideration committee. A recommendation of the reconsideration committee will be presented to the Superintendent of Schools and the Advisory Board of the Office of Lifelong Formation and Education for approval at the next regularly scheduled meeting of the Policies Committee. If the decision of the reconsideration committee is not approved by the Advisory Board, the request will be returned to the reconsideration committee for further review.

FIGURE 5.1
(continued)

REQUEST FOR RECONSIDERATION OF INSTRUCTIONAL MATERIALS

SCHOOL_____

Type of material (e.g. book, video, internet, etc.)_____

Title/Author:_____

Publisher or Producer:_____

Request Initiated by:

Name_____

Phone_____E-mail_____

Address_____

City/State/Zip_____

The following questions are to be answered after the concerned party has read, viewed, or listened to the school library material in the entirety. Please answer the questions on both sides of this form. Add pages as needed.

   1. To what in the material do you object? (Please be specific. Cite pages, etc.)

FIGURE 5.1
(continued)

2. What do you believe is the theme or purpose of this material?

3. What do you feel might be the result of a student using this material?

4. For what age group would you recommend this material?

5. What are the advantages of this material?

6. Would you care to recommend other instructional material that supports the same learning?

Signature _____ Date_____

Date Received_____ Date Reviewed_____

After reviewing your request for_____

_____

We have decided

_____To take no action to remove the material. (Request is denied.)
_____To remove all or part of the challenged material.
_____To limit the use of the challenged material.

FIGURE 5.1
(continued)

PREPARATION FOR RESPONDING TO A CHALLENGE

The first course of action after being presented with a "Request for Reconsideration of Instructional Materials" form by a principal will be to review the procedure concerning review and reevaluation of a library media center resource. In order to prepare for the review committee meeting, the LMS will familiarize herself with the committee's responsibilities and provide any documentation that is necessary to assist in the decision. The following items will be needed for the committee:

1. A statement of the school's selection policy (see page 11)
2. Copies of the challenged material
3. Copies of reputable, professionally prepared reviews of the material and recommendations from reputable selection aids.
4. Copies of "The First Amendment of the Constitution of the United States", "The Library Bill of Rights" and the "Students Right to Read" as mentioned in the policy.

In order to prepare for the meeting, the LMS will review the documents mentioned in the policies. First, in reviewing the Library Bill of Rights from the American Library Association, the role of the library is to provide a variety of materials to its' patrons. The requirements for selecting items to be included in the library collection are interest, information and enlightenment of patrons. Also stated in the Library Bill of Rights is that materials are not to be excluded because of differing opinions. Libraries are also to challenge censorship of materials in the spirit of providing for the enlightenment of their patrons.[7]

The Students' Right to Read indicates that any piece of literature has the possibility to be offensive to someone. This could include religious beliefs, political beliefs, the race or ethnicity of the reader, etc. To deny students the freedom of choice with reading hurts the education of a student, according to the Right to Read statement. If a students' education is hindered, it can also keep them from making choices that would be wiser if they had the freedom to choose what they read. The Right to Read states that teachers should consider the value of the material and the education the student can gain from that piece of literature.[8]

Given the information in these documents, it is clear that the decision of what a child will read is the decision between that child and their parents. A single parent, however, should not be making this decision for the entire student body. Students of the school need to have the opportunity to read many different types of literature and information.

The school media center is at the "forefront of complex and sensitive information issues in today's society."[9] This challenge shows how important it is to be prepared for this situation in every media center. As seen above, this LMC has the policies, book reviews, and ALA documentation to be well prepared for this challenge. The LMS has researched for the committee meeting and can feel good about the information and backing found. It is important, however, to also prepare in attitude for the committee meeting.

Above all, it is essential to remain composed and professional when dealing with this challenge. The challengers and the LMS should not feel they are being personally attacked during the committee meeting. Instead, they should see all parties are taking their concerns seriously and following the established procedures to evaluate the material. Parents believe they are acting in their child's best interests, and the LMS and school need to show the parents that they are striving to act in the interests of all students at the school. Regardless of the outcome, the parents should not feel like they were dismissed by the school and LMS because they will feel they cannot express their opinions in the future. By remaining positive and professional, the LMS can be a positive force towards intellectual freedom for all students.

When the occasion arises that the principal gives the LMS the Challenged Materials form, the first step is to remain calm and rational, remembering to never get personally upset by the challenge or the challenger. The LMS should still be able to smile and act politely to the challenger of the book. Furthermore, the LMS will refrain from denigrating the challenger to other members of the school community. The LMS must act professionally and be a positive force demonstrating a belief in intellectual freedom and the right to read.

---

[7] Library Bill of Rights. American Library Association. 22 July 2009
<http://www.ala.org/ala/aboutala/offices/oif/statementspols/statementsif/librarybillrights.cfm />.
[8] Students' Right to Read. The National Council of Teachers of English. 22 July 2009
<http://www.ncte.org/positions/statements/righttoreadguideline>.
[9] American Association of School Librarians and Association for Educational Communications and Technology. Information Power: Building Partnerships for Learning. Chicago: American Library Association, 1998.

FIGURE 5.1
(continued)

ALA LIBRARY BILL OF RIGHTS

The American Library Association affirms that all libraries are forums for information and ideas, and that the following basic policies should guide their services.

I. Books and other library resources should be provided for the interest, information, and enlightenment of all people of the community the library serves. Materials should not be excluded because of the origin, background, or views of those contributing to their creation.

II. Libraries should provide materials and information presenting all points of view on current and historical issues. Materials should not be proscribed or removed because of partisan or doctrinal disapproval.

III. Libraries should challenge censorship in the fulfillment of their responsibility to provide information and enlightenment.

IV. Libraries should cooperate with all persons and groups concerned with resisting abridgment of free expression and free access to ideas.

V. A person's right to use a library should not be denied or abridged because of origin, age, background, or views.

VI. Libraries which make exhibit spaces and meeting rooms available to the public they serve should make such facilities available on an equitable basis, regardless of the beliefs or affiliations of individuals or groups requesting their use. [10]

Adopted June 18, 1948, by the ALA Council; amended February 2, 1961; January 23, 1980; inclusion of "age" reaffirmed January 23, 1996.

[10] Library Bill of Rights. American Library Association. 22 July 2009
<http://www.ala.org/ala/aboutala/offices/oif/statementspols/statementsif/librarybillrights.cfm />.

FIGURE 5.1
(continued)

NCTE STUDENTS' RIGHT TO READ

The current edition of The Students' Right to Read is an adaptation and updating of the original Council statement, including "Citizen's Request for Reconsideration of a Work," prepared by the Committee on the Right to Read of the National Council of Teachers of English and revised by Ken Donelson.

The right to read, like all rights guaranteed or implied within our constitutional tradition, can be used wisely or foolishly. In many ways, education is an effort to improve the quality of choices open to all students. But to deny the freedom of choice in fear that it may be unwisely used is to destroy the freedom itself. For this reason, we respect the right of individuals to be selective in their own reading. But for the same reason, we oppose efforts of individuals or groups to limit the freedom of choice of others or to impose their own standards or tastes upon the community at large.

The right of any individual not just to read but to read whatever he or she wants to read is basic to a democratic society. This right is based on an assumption that the educated possess judgment and understanding and can be trusted with the determination of their own actions. In effect, the reader is freed from the bonds of chance. The reader is not limited by birth, geographic location, or time, since reading allows meeting people, debating philosophies, and experiencing events far beyond the narrow confines of an individual's own existence.

In selecting books for reading by young people, English teachers consider the contribution which each work may make to the education of the reader, its aesthetic value, its honesty, its readability for a particular group of students, and its appeal to adolescents. English teachers, however, may use different works for different purposes. The criteria for choosing a work to be read by an entire class are somewhat different from the criteria for choosing works to be read by small groups.

For example, a teacher might select John Knowles' A Separate Peace for reading by an entire class, partly because the book has received wide critical recognition, partly because it is relatively short and will keep the attention of many slow readers, and partly because it has proved popular with many students of widely differing abilities. The same teacher, faced with the responsibility of choosing or recommending books for several small groups of students, might select or recommend books as different as Nathaniel Hawthorne's The Scarlet Letter, Jack Schaefer's Shane, Alexander Solzhenitsyn's One Day in the Life of Ivan Denisovitch, Pierre Boulle's The Bridge over the River Kwai, Charles Dickens' Great Expectations, or Paul Zindel's The Pigman, depending upon the abilities and interests of the students in each group.

And the criteria for suggesting books to individuals or for recommending something worth reading for a student who casually stops by after class are different from those for selecting material for a class or group. But the teacher selects, not censors, books. Selection implies that a teacher is free to choose this or that work, depending upon the purpose to be achieved and the student or class in question, but a book selected this year may be ignored next year, and the reverse. Censorship implies that certain works are not open to selection, this year or any year.

Wallace Stevens once wrote, "Literature is the better part of life. To this it seems inevitably necessary to add, provided life is the better part of literature." Students and parents have the right to demand that education today keep students in touch with the reality of the world outside the classroom. Much of classic literature asks questions as valid and significant today as when the literature first appeared, questions like "What is the nature of humanity?" "Why do people praise individuality and practice conformity?" "What do people need for a good life?" and "What is the nature of the good person?" But youth is the age of revolt. To pretend otherwise is to ignore a reality made clear to young people and adults alike on television and radio, in newspapers and magazines. English teachers must be free to employ books, classic or contemporary, which do not lie to the young about the perilous but wondrous times we live in, books which talk of the fears, hopes, joys, and frustrations people experience, books about people not only as they are but as they can be. English teachers forced through the pressures of censorship to use only safe or antiseptic works are placed in the morally and intellectually untenable position of lying to their students about the nature and condition of mankind.

The teacher must exercise care to select or recommend works for class reading and group discussion. One of the most important responsibilities of the English teacher is developing rapport and respect among students. Respect for the uniqueness and potential of the individual, an important facet of the study of literature, should be emphasized in the English class. Literature classes should reflect the cultural contributions of many minority groups in the United States, just as they should acquaint students with contributions from the peoples of Asia, Africa, and Latin America.[11]

---

[11] Students' Right to Read. The National Council of Teachers of English. 22 July 2009
<http://www.ncte.org/positions/statements/righttoreadguideline>.

FIGURE 5.1
(continued)

ALA FREEDOM TO READ STATEMENT

The freedom to read is essential to our democracy. It is continuously under attack. Private groups and public authorities in various parts of the country are working to remove or limit access to reading materials, to censor content in schools, to label "controversial" views, to distribute lists of "objectionable" books or authors, and to purge libraries. These actions apparently rise from a view that our national tradition of free expression is no longer valid; that censorship and suppression are needed to counter threats to safety or national security, as well as to avoid the subversion of politics and the corruption of morals. We, as individuals devoted to reading and as librarians and publishers responsible for disseminating ideas, wish to assert the public interest in the preservation of the freedom to read.

Most attempts at suppression rest on a denial of the fundamental premise of democracy: that the ordinary individual, by exercising critical judgment, will select the good and reject the bad. We trust Americans to recognize propaganda and misinformation, and to make their own decisions about what they read and believe. We do not believe they are prepared to sacrifice their heritage of a free press in order to be "protected" against what others think may be bad for them. We believe they still favor free enterprise in ideas and expression.

These efforts at suppression are related to a larger pattern of pressures being brought against education, the press, art and images, films, broadcast media, and the Internet. The problem is not only one of actual censorship. The shadow of fear cast by these pressures leads, we suspect, to an even larger voluntary curtailment of expression by those who seek to avoid controversy or unwelcome scrutiny by government officials.

Such pressure toward conformity is perhaps natural to a time of accelerated change. And yet suppression is never more dangerous than in such a time of social tension. Freedom has given the United States the elasticity to endure strain. Freedom keeps open the path of novel and creative solutions, and enables change to come by choice. Every silencing of a heresy, every enforcement of an orthodoxy, diminishes the toughness and resilience of our society and leaves it the less able to deal with controversy and difference.

Now as always in our history, reading is among our greatest freedoms. The freedom to read and write is almost the only means for making generally available ideas or manners of expression that can initially command only a small audience. The written word is the natural medium for the new idea and the untried voice from which come the original contributions to social growth. It is essential to the extended discussion that serious thought requires, and to the accumulation of knowledge and ideas into organized collections.

We believe that free communication is essential to the preservation of a free society and a creative culture. We believe that these pressures toward conformity present the danger of limiting the range and variety of inquiry and expression on which our democracy and our culture depend. We believe that every American community must jealously guard the freedom to publish and to circulate, in order to preserve its own freedom to read. We believe that publishers and librarians have a profound responsibility to give validity to that freedom to read by making it possible for the readers to choose freely from a variety of offerings.

The freedom to read is guaranteed by the Constitution. Those with faith in free people will stand firm on these constitutional guarantees of essential rights and will exercise the responsibilities that accompany these rights. We therefore affirm these propositions:

1. *It is in the public interest for publishers and librarians to make available the widest diversity of views and expressions, including those that are unorthodox, unpopular, or considered dangerous by the majority.*

Creative thought is by definition new, and what is new is different. The bearer of every new thought is a rebel until that idea is refined and tested. Totalitarian systems attempt to maintain themselves in power by the ruthless suppression of any concept that challenges the established orthodoxy. The power of a democratic system to adapt to change is vastly strengthened by the freedom of its citizens to choose widely from among conflicting opinions offered freely to them. To stifle every nonconformist idea at birth would mark the end of the democratic process. Furthermore, only through the constant activity of weighing and selecting can the democratic mind attain the strength demanded by times like these. We need to know not only what we believe but why we believe it.

2. *Publishers, librarians, and booksellers do not need to endorse every idea or presentation they make available. It would conflict with the public interest for them to establish their own political, moral, or aesthetic views as a standard for determining what should be published or circulated.*

Publishers and librarians serve the educational process by helping to make available knowledge and ideas required for the growth of the mind and the increase of learning. They do not foster education by imposing as mentors the patterns of their own thought. The people should have the freedom to read and consider a broader range of ideas than those that may be held

Archdiocese of Louisville
Library Media Guidelines

August 2009
Page 26

FIGURE 5.1
(continued)

by any single librarian or publisher or government or church. It is wrong that what one can read should be confined to what another thinks proper.

3. *It is contrary to the public interest for publishers or librarians to bar access to writings on the basis of the personal history or political affiliations of the author.*

No art or literature can flourish if it is to be measured by the political views or private lives of its creators. No society of free people can flourish that draws up lists of writers to whom it will not listen, whatever they may have to say.

4. *There is no place in our society for efforts to coerce the taste of others, to confine adults to the reading matter deemed suitable for adolescents, or to inhibit the efforts of writers to achieve artistic expression.*

To some, much of modern expression is shocking. But is not much of life itself shocking? We cut off literature at the source if we prevent writers from dealing with the stuff of life. Parents and teachers have a responsibility to prepare the young to meet the diversity of experiences in life to which they will be exposed, as they have a responsibility to help them learn to think critically for themselves. These are affirmative responsibilities, not to be discharged simply by preventing them from reading works for which they are not yet prepared. In these matters values differ, and values cannot be legislated; nor can machinery be devised that will suit the demands of one group without limiting the freedom of others.

5. *It is not in the public interest to force a reader to accept the prejudgment of a label characterizing any expression or its author as subversive or dangerous.*

The ideal of labeling presupposes the existence of individuals or groups with wisdom to determine by authority what is good or bad for others. It presupposes that individuals must be directed in making up their minds about the ideas they examine. But Americans do not need others to do their thinking for them.

6. *It is the responsibility of publishers and librarians, as guardians of the people's freedom to read, to contest encroachments upon that freedom by individuals or groups seeking to impose their own standards or tastes upon the community at large; and by the government whenever it seeks to reduce or deny public access to public information.*

It is inevitable in the give and take of the democratic process that the political, the moral, or the aesthetic concepts of an individual or group will occasionally collide with those of another individual or group. In a free society individuals are free to determine for themselves what they wish to read, and each group is free to determine what it will recommend to its freely associated members. But no group has the right to take the law into its own hands, and to impose its own concept of politics or morality upon other members of a democratic society. Freedom is no freedom if it is accorded only to the accepted and the inoffensive. Further, democratic societies are more safe, free, and creative when the free flow of public information is not restricted by governmental prerogative or self-censorship.

7. *It is the responsibility of publishers and librarians to give full meaning to the freedom to read by providing books that enrich the quality and diversity of thought and expression. By the exercise of this affirmative responsibility, they can demonstrate that the answer to a "bad" book is a good one, the answer to a "bad" idea is a good one.*

The freedom to read is of little consequence when the reader cannot obtain matter fit for that reader's purpose. What is needed is not only the absence of restraint, but the positive provision of opportunity for the people to read the best that has been thought and said. Books are the major channel by which the intellectual inheritance is handed down, and the principal means of its testing and growth. The defense of the freedom to read requires of all publishers and librarians the utmost of their faculties, and deserves of all Americans the fullest of their support.

We state these propositions neither lightly nor as easy generalizations. We here stake out a lofty claim for the value of the written word. We do so because we believe that it is possessed of enormous variety and usefulness, worthy of cherishing and keeping free. We realize that the application of these propositions may mean the dissemination of ideas and manners of expression that are repugnant to many persons. We do not state these propositions in the comfortable belief that what people read is unimportant. We believe rather that what people read is deeply important; that ideas can be dangerous; but that the suppression of ideas is fatal to a democratic society. Freedom itself is a dangerous way of life, but it is ours.

This statement was originally issued in May of 1953 by the Westchester Conference of the American Library Association and the American Book Publishers Council, which in 1970 consolidated with the American Educational Publishers Institute to become the Association of American Publishers.[12]

---

[12] "Freedom to Read Statement." American Library Association. 2008. 22 July 2009.
<http://www.ala.org/ala/aboutala/offices/oif/statementspols/ftrstatement/freedomreadstatement.cfm>.

FIGURE 5.1
(continued)

ALA FREEDOM TO VIEW STATEMENT

The **FREEDOM TO VIEW**, along with the freedom to speak, to hear, and to read, is protected by the First Amendment to the Constitution of the United States. In a free society, there is no place for censorship of any medium of expression. Therefore these principles are affirmed:

1. To provide the broadest access to film, video, and other audiovisual materials because they are a means for the communication of ideas. Liberty of circulation is essential to insure the constitutional guarantee of freedom of expression.

2. To protect the confidentiality of all individuals and institutions using film, video, and other audiovisual materials.

3. To provide film, video, and other audiovisual materials which represent a diversity of views and expression. Selection of a work does not constitute or imply agreement with or approval of the content.

4. To provide a diversity of viewpoints without the constraint of labeling or prejudging film, video, or other audiovisual materials on the basis of the moral, religious, or political beliefs of the producer or filmmaker or on the basis of controversial content.

5. To contest vigorously, by all lawful means, every encroachment upon the public's freedom to view.

This statement was originally drafted by the Freedom to View Committee of the American Film and Video Association (formerly the Educational Film Library Association) and was adopted by the AFVA Board of Directors in February 1979. This statement was updated and approved by the AFVA Board of Directors in 1989.

Endorsed January 10, 1990, by the ALA Council[13]

---

[13] "Freedom to View Statement." American Library Association. 2008. 22 July 2009.
<http://www.ala.org/ala/aboutala/offices/oif/statementspols/ftvstatement/freedomviewstatement.cfm>.

FIGURE 5.1
(continued)

University of Utah

The policy at the University of Utah maps its policy to purpose and scope, provides extensive definitions of terms, and brings a focus to both Section 107 Fair Use and Section 108 Libraries & Archives. See figure 5.2.

Policy 7-013: Copyright Policy: Copying of Copyrighted Works

I. Purpose and Scope

To declare the university's Policy regarding compliance with U.S. Copyright Law.

This Policy applies to all University personnel (including faculty, staff, and other employees), all students, and all academic and administrative units of the University

II. Definitions

These definitions apply for the limited purposes of this Policy and any associated University Regulations. Terms used in this Policy which also are used within Title 17, United States Code (see 17 U.S.C., Section 101), are intended to have the same meaning for purposes of this Policy as they have within that Code.

A. Audiovisual works -- are works that consist of a series of related images which are intrinsically intended to be shown by the use of machines or devices such as projectors, viewers, or electronic equipment, together with accompanying sounds, if any, regardless of the nature of the material objects, such as films or tapes, in which the works are embodied.

B. Copies -- are material objects, other than phonorecords, in which a work is fixed by any method now known or later developed, and from which the work can be perceived, reproduced, or otherwise communicated, either directly or with the aid of a machine or device. The term "copies" includes the material object, other than a phonorecord, in which the work is first fixed.

C. Copyright owner -- with respect to any one of the exclusive rights comprised in a copyright, refers to the owner of that particular right.

D. Fair use -- is a reasonable noninfringing use, including reproduction, of copyrighted material for such Purposes as criticism, comment, news reporting, teaching, scholarship or research, as determined from consideration of all relevant circumstances, including (1) the Purpose or character of the use, e.g., for commercial Purposes or for nonprofit educational Purposes, (2) the nature of the copyrighted work, (3) the amount and substantiality of the portion used in relation to the copyrighted work as a whole, and (4) the effect of the use upon the potential

FIGURE 5.2

Copying of Copyrighted Works. *University of Utah, https://regulations.utah.edu/research/7-013.php.*

market for or value of the copyrighted work.

E. Literary works -- are works, other than audiovisual works, expressed in words, numbers, or other verbal or numerical symbols or indicia, regardless of the nature of the material objects, such as books, periodicals, manuscripts, phonorecords, film, tapes, discs, or cards, in which they are embodied.

F. Phonorecords -- are material objects in which sounds, other that those accompanying a motion picture or other audiovisual work, are fixed by any method now known or later developed, and from which the sounds can be perceived, reproduced, or otherwise communicated, either directly or with the aid of a machine or device. The term "phonorecords" includes the material object in which the sounds are first fixed.

G. Publication -- is the distribution of copies or phonorecords of a work to the public by sale or other transfer of ownership, or by rental, lease, or lending. The offering to distribute copies or phonorecords to a group of persons for Purposes of further distribution, public performance, or public display, constitutes publication. A public performance or display of a work does not of itself constitute publication.

H. University -- unless the context otherwise requires, includes the University of Utah institution and its officers and employees acting in the scope of their office or employment.

I. Work -- means a work of authorship that is capable of copyright protection, including literary, musical, dramatic, choreographic, pictorial, graphic, sculptural, motion picture, audiovisual, and sound recording works.

J. Academic use -- means a use that relates to or is consistent with the mission of the University.

III. Policy

A. General Principles--- Exclusive Rights, and Permissible Uses of Copyrighted Materials in Furtherance of the University's Academic Missions

1. University faculty and staff members and other personnel are expected to recognize and observe the exclusive rights of copyright owners.

2. This Policy shall be construed liberally to carry out the dual purposes for which specific limitations upon these exclusive rights were written into the law:

a. to promote and facilitate academic uses of copyrighted materials, and

b. to reduce incidences of copyright infringement.

FIGURE 5.2
(continued)

3. Under federal law (17 U.S.C., Section 106), the owner of copyright has the exclusive rights to do and to authorize any of the following:

   a. to reproduce the copyrighted work in copies or phonorecords;

   b. to prepare derivative works based upon the copyrighted work;

   c. to distribute copies or phonorecords of the copyrighted work to the public by sale or other transfer of ownership, or by rental, lease, or lending;

   d. in the case of literary, musical, dramatic, and choreographic works, pantomimes, and pictorial, graphic, or sculptural works, including the individual images of a motion picture or other audiovisual work, to perform or display the copyrighted work publicly.

B. Copying for Personal Use

   The making of a single reproduction or phonorecording of copyrighted matter, including works contained in the collections of the university libraries or archives or obtained by interlibrary loan, is permitted if:

   1. The University reasonably believes that the reproduction is made without any purpose of direct or indirect commercial advantage;

   2. the copy or phonorecord will become the property of the user;

   3. the university has no notice that the copy or phonorecord will be used for any purpose other than private study, scholarship, or research; and

   4. such reproduction or phonorecording, and the intended use to be made of it, constitute fair use.

C. Copying for Academic Use

   The reproduction or phonorecording of copyrighted works for academic purposes, such as criticism, comment, teaching, scholarship, or research, is permitted, if fair use standards for permissible copying are observed:The factors to determine and document whether a use is fair include:

   1. Purpose and character of the use, including whether such use is of a commercial nature or is for nonprofit educational purposes;

   2. Nature of the copyrighted work;Amount and substantiality of the portion used in relation to the copyrighted work as a whole;Effect of the use upon the potential market for or value of

FIGURE 5.2
(continued)

the copyrighted work.

D. Digital Content and Transmission for Teaching

1. Digital content which includes any copyrighted work may be digitally transmitted (shared) among course instructors and students enrolled in a particular course offered by the University, under the following conditions:

   a. The use of the copyright work constitutes a fair use,

   b. Access to the digital content is limited only to those students enrolled in the course for which the content has been obtained and only during the semester or other pertinent time period the course is offered; and

   c. access to the digital content is controlled by password protection or an equivalent security measure.

E. Copying by University Libraries

1. General reserve desks may circulate single reproduction copies of library-owned copyrighted materials, provided that in the preparation of such circulating copies, library personnel do not exceed the standards for permissible copying under the law of fair use.

2. With respect to interlibrary loans, university libraries as borrowing libraries shall keep and retain records of filled loan requests for three full years following the end of the calendar year in which the requests were made in order to insure that during said period of three years:

   a. The library did not request and receive more than five articles from any copyrighted periodical title published within the five years immediately prior to the date of a request; and

   b. the library did not request and receive more than five copies of or from any given copyrighted work, including a collection of copyrighted works, during the entire period such material was protected by copyright.

3. University libraries as lending libraries may make isolated and unrelated reproductions of a single copy of the same copyrighted materials on separate occasions as long as the libraries and their personnel are not aware of and have no reason to believe they are engaging in related or concerted reproduction of multiple copies.

4. University libraries shall refuse:

FIGURE 5.2
(continued)

a. to fill an interlibrary loan request where prior contractual obligations prohibit copying of such copyrighted material;

b. to honor a request from a borrowing library which has not verified on its order form that the request conforms to the copyright law and guidelines.

5. For the purpose of preserving and maintaining library collections, university libraries are permitted to make:

a. facsimile reproductions of unpublished works that are currently in the library-owned collection for purposes of preservation, security, or deposit in another library; and

b. a copy of published copyrighted work to replace a work that is damaged, deteriorating, lost or stolen, if:

  i. the library determines, after a reasonable effort, that an unused replacement cannot be obtained at a fair price, and

  ii. the copy includes a notice of copyright.

F. Prohibitions

In addition to compliance with applicable limitations on uses of copyrighted materials as provided herein, faculty and staff and other University personnel are expected to refrain from any of the following actions:

1. Books and periodicals

Unless authorized in writing by the owner of the copyright to any book or periodical:

a. Copying may not be used to create, or to replace or substitute for, anthologies, compilations or collections of copyrighted works. Replacement or substitution may occur whether copies of various works or excerpts therefrom are accumulated or are reproduced and used separately.

b. There shall be no copying of or from copyrighted works intended to be "consumable" in the course of study or of teaching, such as workbooks, exercises, standardized tests, test booklets and answer sheets, and like consumable material.

c. Copying may not:

  i. be used as a substitute for the purchase of books, publishers' reprints or periodicals;

FIGURE 5.2
(continued)

    ii. be repeated with respect to the same item by the same course instructor in successive semesters or sessions without fair use documentation.

  d. No charge may be made to a student for a single copy of copyrighted materials beyond the actual cost of reproduction.

2. Educational uses of music

  Unless authorized in writing by the owner of the copyright to any music:

  a. Copying may not be used to create, or replace or substitute for, anthologies, compilations or collective works.

  b. There shall be no copying of or from works intended to be "consumable" in the course of study or of teaching, such as

  c. workbooks, exercises, standardized tests and answer sheets, and like material.

  d. Copying may not be used for the purpose of performance, except as permitted as a fair use.

  e. Copying may not be used as a substitute for the purchase of music, except as permitted as a fair use.

  f. Copying is not permitted without inclusion of the copyright notice which appears on the printed copy of the music.

  g. [Users should also refer to University Rule 4-002A regarding illegal file sharing.]

3. Off-air recording

  Unless authorized in writing by the owner of the copyright in any television program:

  a. Television programs may not be regularly recorded in anticipation of instructor requests by any media services unit of the University.

4. Computer Programs (Software)

  Unless authorized in writing by the owner of the copyright in any computer program:

  a. Copying of computer programs may not be used as a substitute for purchase.

G. Notices and Warnings to Prevent Copyright Infringement

1. A "Display Warning of Copyright" conforming to requirements specified by the Register of

FIGURE 5.2
(continued)

Copyrights shall be displayed prominently, in such a manner and location as to be clearly visible, legible, and comprehensible to a casual observer within the immediate vicinity of each place on the University campus at which orders are accepted for the making of copies or phonorecords of copyrighted materials.

2. An "Order Warning of Copyright" conforming to requirements specified by the Register of Copyrights shall be included on printed forms used by library patrons for ordering copies or phonorecords of copyrighted materials.

3. All unsupervised reproducing equipment located in public areas on University premises shall display a notice that the making of a copy of copyrighted materials may be subject to the copyright law. The notice is to be affixed on the equipment so that it is readily apparent to a person making a copy.

H. Responsibilities for Notices and Enforcement

1. Posting Notices and Warnings

   Responsibility for assuring that required notices and warnings are properly posted or affixed as required under this Policy rests with the cognizant vice presidents.

2. Enforcement of Minimum Compliance Standards

   a. Development of operating practices to assure compliance with minimum standards for copying rests with line management personnel, under the direction of the cognizant vice presidents.

   b. Operating practices for complying with legal requirements relating to performances of copyrighted musical, literary, and dramatic works shall be initiated by the relevant university operating units under the direction of the cognizant vice president

   c. Payment of royalties for copying or performance of copyrighted works, where required in the course of university business, shall be charged to regularly budgeted departmental funds.

   d. In the event that a determination of copyright infringement by a court of competent jurisdiction results in the imposition of a final judgment imposing damages, costs, or other penalties upon the university, or upon any university officer or employee for acts or omissions in the scope of employment, any resulting loss to the university shall, except where otherwise required by law, be payable from funds budgeted for the use of the

FIGURE 5.2
(continued)

responsible operating unit if such loss was reasonably avoidable by compliance with this Policy.

3. Questions as to the interpretation of this Policy, or as to other aspects of copyright law, should be addressed to the Office of General Counsel or J. Willard Marriott Library.

[Note: Parts IV-VII of this Regulation (and all other University Regulations) are Regulations Resource Information – the contents of which are not approved by the Academic Senate or Board of Trustees, and are to be updated from time to time as determined appropriate by the cognizant Policy Officer and the Institutional Policy Committee, as per Policy 1-001 and Rule 1-001.]

IV. Rules, Procedures, Guidelines, Forms, and other related resources.

A. Rules [reserved]

B. Procedures [reserved]

C. Guidelines [reserved]

D. Forms [reserved]

E. Other related resource materials [reserved]

V. References.

Policy 7-002, Patents, Inventions and Copyrights.

Policy 3-112 Campus Printing Policy.

Rule 4-002A: Compliance with Illegal File Sharing Provisions of the HEOA (Higher Education Opportunity Act)

VI. Contacts:

The designated contact officials for this Policy are:

A. Policy Owner (primary contact person for questions and advice): University Librarian.

B. Policy Officer: Chief Academic Officer.

These officials are designated by the University President or delegee, with assistance of the Institutional Policy Committee, to have the following roles and authority, as provided in

FIGURE 5.2
(continued)

University Rule 1-001:

"A 'Policy Officer' will be assigned by the President for each University Policy, and will typically be someone at the executive level of the University (i.e., the President and his/her Cabinet Officers). The assigned Policy Officer is authorized to allow exceptions to the Policy in appropriate cases.... "

"The Policy Officer will identify an 'Owner' for each Policy. The Policy Owner is an expert on the Policy topic who may respond to questions about, and provide interpretation of the Policy; and will typically be someone reporting to an executive level position (as defined above), but may be any other person to whom the President or a Vice President has delegated such authority for a specified area of University operations. The Owner has primary responsibility for maintaining the relevant portions of the Regulations Library... . [and] bears the responsibility for determining -requirements of particular Policies... ." University Rule 1-001-III-B & E

VII. History

Renumbering: Renumbered as Policy 7-013 effective 9/15/2008, formerly known as PPM 6-5.

Revision History:

A. Current version-- University Policy 7-013 Revision 3. Approved by Academic Senate: January 6, 2014. Approved by the Board of Trustees: January 14, 2014 , with the designated effective date of January 14, 2014.

   Editorial revisions to current version: [Reserved]

   Background (/research/revisions_7/7-013R3%20Background.pdf) information on Revision 3.

B. Earlier versions.

   Revision 2 (/research/revisions_7/Policy%207-013.R2.pdf).   Effective dates January 16, 1978 to January 13, 2014. Editorially revised Sept. 27, 1985.

FIGURE 5.2
(continued)

Snow College Libraries

The copyright policy for Snow College Libraries begins with a purpose statement and definitions. It incorporates three exceptions: Section 107 Fair Use, Section 108 Libraries & Archives, and Section 110(1) Face-to-Face Teaching. Two distinguishing elements of the policy include express guidance on copying for those with disabilities and the public performance and display of movies in the library. See sections 4.4 and 4.5 in figure 5.3.

SUBJECT: LIBRARIES COPYRIGHT POLICY

1. PURPOSE
   1.1. The Snow College Libraries are dedicated to providing an environment where learning occurs. The library provides research instruction and quality curriculum supporting information sources in the most appropriate formats.
   1.2. As many of the materials provided by the Libraries in support of its role and mission are copyrighted, this Policy provides guidance on the application of copyright law to materials and resources provided by the College Libraries.

2. DEFINITIONS
   2.1. Exclusive Rights: Federal law (primarily the Copyright Act of 1976 and the Digital Millennium Copyright Act of 1998 found in Title 17 of the United States Code) protects original works of authorship through the U.S. Copyright Act. The owner of a copyright under the Copyright Act has the exclusive rights to do and to authorize any of the following:
      2.1.1. To reproduce the copyrighted work in copies or phonorecords.
      2.1.2. To prepare derivative works based upon the copyrighted work.
      2.1.3. To distribute copies or phonorecords of the copyrighted work to the public by sale or other transfer of ownership, or by rental lease, or lending.
      2.1.4. In the case of literary, musical, dramatic, and choreographic works, pantomimes, and motion pictures and other audiovisual works, to perform the copyrighted work publicly.
      2.1.5. In the case of literary, musical, dramatic, and choreographic works, pantomimes, and pictorial, graphic, or sculptural works, including the individual images of a motion picture or other audiovisual work, to display the copyrighted work publicly.
      2.1.6. In the case of sound recordings, to perform the copyrighted work publicly by means of a digital audio transmission.
   2.2. Fair Use Exception: A reasonable noninfringing use, including reproduction, of copyrighted material for such purposes as criticism, comment, news reporting, teaching (including multiple copies for classroom use), scholarship or research, as determined from consideration of all relevant circumstances, including (1) the purpose and character of the use, including whether such use is of a commercial nature or is for nonprofit educational purposes; (2) the nature of the copyrighted work; (3) the amount and substantiality of the portion used in relation to the copyrighted work as a whole (generally less than 10% or one chapter of a book); and (4) the effect of the use upon the potential market for or value of the copyrighted work.
   2.3. Library & Archives Exception: It is not an infringement of copyright for a library or archives, or any of its employees acting within the scope of their employment, to reproduce no more than one copy of a work or to distribute such copy or phonorecord under certain conditions.
   2.4. Face-to-Face Teaching Exception: It is not an infringement of copyright to perform or display a copyrighted work a work by instructors or pupils in the course of face-to-face teaching activities of a nonprofit educational institution, in a classroom or similar place devoted to instruction, of a lawfully made copy.
   2.5. Copying: Making a reproduction of materials including paper copies and electronic versions.
   2.6. Other definitions are as stated in 17 USC 101.

FIGURE 5.3
Libraries Copyright Policy. *Snow College Libraries.*

3. POLICY
   3.1. Snow College Libraries protect the rights of holders of copyright in accord with Federal and state law, rules and regulations ("law"). Libraries materials may not be copied or used except in accord with the law and this Policy and Procedures.
   3.2. Snow College Libraries abides by disability and accommodation rules and regulations and this Policy and Procedures shall be implemented in accord with those.

4. PROCEDURES
   4.1. Copying of copyrighted works by library employees and patrons within the library.
      4.1.1. General reserve desks may circulate single reproduction copies of library-owned copyrighted materials, provided that in the preparation of such circulating copies, library personnel do not exceed the standards for permissible copying under the law of fair use. A copy shall include a notice of copyright as found in the original or a notice that the work may be protected by copyright.
      4.1.2. With respect to interlibrary loans, Snow College libraries as borrowing libraries shall keep and retain records of filled loan requests for three full years following the end of the calendar year in which the requests were made in order to insure that during said period of three years:
         4.1.2.1. The library did not request and receive more than five articles from any copyrighted periodical title published within the five years immediately prior to the date of a request; and
         4.1.2.2. the library did not request and receive more than five copies of or from any given copyrighted work, including a collection of copyrighted works, during the entire period such material was protected by copyright.
      4.1.3. Snow College libraries as lending libraries may make isolated and unrelated reproductions of a single copy of the same copyrighted materials on separate occasions as long as the libraries and their personnel are not aware of and have no reason to believe they are engaging in related or concerted reproduction of multiple copies.
      4.1.4. College libraries shall refuse:
         4.1.4.1. to fill an interlibrary loan request where prior contractual obligations prohibit copying of such copyrighted material;
         4.1.4.2. to honor a request from a borrowing library which has not verified on its order form that the request conforms to the copyright law and guidelines.
      4.1.5. For the purpose of preserving and maintaining library collections, College libraries are permitted to make:
         4.1.5.1. facsimile reproductions of unpublished works that are currently in the library-owned collection for purposes of preservation, security, or deposit in another library; and
         4.1.5.2. a copy of published copyrighted work to replace a work that is damaged, deteriorating, lost or stolen, if:
            4.1.5.2.1. the library determines, after a reasonable effort, that an unused replacement cannot be obtained at a fair price, and
            4.1.5.2.2. the copy includes a notice of copyright.
   4.2. Copying for Personal Use
      4.2.1. Copies for personal use may only be made in accord with the Fair Use Exception.

FIGURE 5.3
(continued)

4.3. Copying for Classroom Use

    4.3.1. Copies for classroom use may only be made in accord with the Fair Use Exception. For guidance on this topic see sections *How does fair use apply to photocopying of course materials?* and *How does fair use apply to use of third-party materials on a course website?* found in the Harvard Office of General Counsel publication **Copyright and Fair Use** found at https://ogc.harvard.edu/pages/copyright-and-fair-use (Copyright © 2016 President and Fellows of Harvard College).

4.4. Copying for those with disabilities and in aid of accommodations.

    4.4.1. Copies for those with disabilities and in aid of accommodations may be made in accord with disability law, rules and regulations.

4.5. Performance or display of copyrighted works in the library.

    4.5.1. The performance or display of copyrighted works may occur in the library in the course of face-to-face teaching activities in an area such as a classroom, study area or auditorium devoted to instruction including showing a lawfully made copy of a full-length movie, playing a lawfully made recording of a song, or showing a lawfully obtained image without a license.

FIGURE 5.3
(continued)

LIBRARIES PART OF GOVERNMENT OR PUBLIC ENTITIES

Somerset County Library System

Somerset County Library System provides a straightforward, readable policy. Mission and purpose set the stage, followed by a single but comprehensive line about employees adhering to U.S. Copyright Law. Given the library's mission, more details about Section 107 and 108 could be considered. See figure 5.4.

Somerset County Library System – Policy Manual

CHAPTER IV -- OPERATING POLICIES

M. Collection Management Policy

A. Introduction

    a. The mission of SCLSNJ is to partner with our residents to connect, to explore, to share and to discover. We provide library services and resources that help people in Somerset County expand their knowledge and talents, make informed decisions, enrich their leisure hours, and enhance their daily lives. To fulfill this mission, SCLSNJ provides materials and information to support a wide range of community and individual interests.

    b. SCLSNJ is a library system of ten branches serving fifteen communities. Library staff work to provide a strong collection of materials and information in a variety of formats that reflect diverse points of view, which are carefully selected in response to and in anticipation of the needs and expectations of users of all ages.

B. Purpose

    a. The SCLSNJ Collection Management Plan guides staff in, and informs the public of, the process upon which collection development decisions are based. The Collection Management Plan consists of this policy and various selection and collection management procedures used by the staff. The criteria of the policy and procedures are designed to help the staff develop library collections that support the roles outlined in the SCLSNJ Strategic Plan.

    b. Collection development is understood to include both acquiring new materials for SCLSNJ libraries and evaluating existing materials for continued relevance to the collections.

C. Intellectual Freedom

    a. SCLSNJ is committed to the protection of the democratic ideal of the free flow of information and ideas, and to the right of free access to information for all individuals.

    b. SCLSNJ subscribes to the principles outlined in the American Library Association's Library Bill of Rights, Freedom to Read Statement, and "Freedom to View Statement"

        i. http://www.ala.org/advocacy/sites/ala.org.advocacy/files/content/intfreedom/librarybill/lbor.pdf.

        ii. http://www.ala.org/advocacy/intfreedom/statementspols/freedomreadstatement

        iii. http://www.ala.org/vrt/professionalresources/vrtresources/freedomtoview.

    c. SCLSNJ collection management decisions are based solely on the merit of an item as to whether it meets the goals of the SCLSNJ mission and the needs and interests of a diverse community. Inclusion of an item in a library's collection is not an endorsement of its content, and the library recognizes that some materials

FIGURE 5.4

Collection Management Policy. *Somerset County Library, https://s40873y1pyb1ozqsg275sisu-wpengine.netdna-ssl.com/wp-content/uploads/M-Collection-Management-Policy.pdf.*

may be considered controversial by some individuals.

    d. Library users are each responsible for determining what materials are appropriate in light of their own personal needs and values. Parents and legal guardians have full responsibility for overseeing their children's use of library materials.

D. Copyright

    a. SCLSNJ supports and adheres to all United States Copyright laws and regulations.

E. Selection and Evaluation of Library Materials

    a. SCLSNJ acquires materials in a variety of formats: print, digital, video, and audio. The same work may be acquired in more than one format.

    b. SCLSNJ continuously reviews and revises the mix of formats it acquires in response to the development of new media and to the demonstrated and perceived needs of its users.

    c. SCLSNJ staff utilizes professional judgment and expertise in making collection development decisions, including decisions about choosing titles and formats, identifying quantities for purchase, and selecting locations for materials. Anticipated demand, community interests, strengths and weaknesses of the existing collections, system-wide availability, physical space limitations, purchasing availability, and budget limitations are all factors taken into consideration.

    d. SCLSNJ does not purchase textbooks in order to supply students with textbooks for required academic courses. Textbooks may be purchased if they provide information that cannot be found in another resource and because that will meet an anticipated need.

    e. The SCLSNJ world language collection is designed to meet the needs of native speakers of a variety of languages, as well as people interested in language study. Each branch in the system will house materials in languages that reflect local language populations within its service area.

    f. SCLSNJ also collects materials created by Somerset County authors. These self-published or small press items may not meet criteria established for the main-stream and journal reviewed items typically collected by the system. However, the Strategic Plan promotes our partnership with our local authors, so we collect locally produced resources and works for future use. Somerset County authors, illustrators, musicians and filmmakers are encouraged to donate at least one copy of their work to SCLSNJ through their local branch. Materials will be reviewed by local branch staff and Collection Management staff to assess which collection (juvenile, young adult or adult) and location is the best fit for each work. Then the item will be added, made searchable in our catalog and made available for patrons to use.

    g. Standards of professional librarianship and the following criteria are employed for selection and reevaluation decisions:

        i. Content

            1. Professional reviews;

1

FIGURE 5.4
(continued)

2. Demonstrated or perceived interest, need, or demand by library users or potential users, status of existing holdings in relation to customer demand;
3. Currency, contemporary significance, popular interest or historic importance;
4. Relevance to the experiences and contributions of the diverse populations served in Somerset County;
5. Representation of controversial and/or diverse points of view;
6. Quality, including awards received, accuracy, clarity, reputation or qualification of the author or publisher, including authority and competence;
7. Relation to existing collections;
8. Value of resource in relation to its cost.

    ii. Format:
1. Accessibility, durability, physical suitability, and ease of use;
2. Additional format criteria are considered when selecting digital content, including: accessibility; ease of use; and equipment; training; and technology needed;
3. Cost in relation to use and/or potential to enhance the collection;
4. Demand.

h. SCLSNJ does not purchase textbooks in order to supply students with textbooks for required academic courses. Textbooks may be purchased if they provide information that cannot be found in another resource and because that will meet an anticipated need.

i. Special Considerations
    i. The SCLSNJ world language collection is designed to meet the needs of native speakers of a variety of languages, as well as people interested in language study. Each branch in the system will house materials in languages that reflect local language populations within its service area.
    ii. SCLSNJ also collects materials created by Somerset County authors. *While* these self-published or small press items may not meet criteria established for the mainstream and journal reviewed items typically collected by the system, we collect locally produced resources and works for future use. Somerset County authors, illustrators, musicians and filmmakers are encouraged to donate at least one copy of their work to SCLSNJ through their local branch. Materials will be reviewed by local branch staff and Collection Development staff to assess which collection (juvenile, young adult or adult) and location is the best fit for each work.

F. Collection Evaluation and Management

a. The collections of the SCLSNJ branches are continually evaluated according to the criteria set forth in the SCLSNJ Collection Management Policy, the library system's vision, mission, and values statements, and the priorities outlined in the SCLSNJ Strategic Plan. Once in the collection, materials are regularly assessed with regard to their accuracy, relevance, physical condition, and use by the public.

2

FIGURE 5.4
(continued)

Worn, damaged, unused, and obsolete materials will be withdrawn from the collection and disposed of according to SCLSNJ procedures.

b. Through ongoing quantitative and qualitative methods, the Collection Development team and branch librarians monitor our collections to see that they are serving the needs of the individual branches, as well as of the system.

G. Gifts and Donations

a. SCLSNJ accepts donations of materials, and donations of money designated for the purchase of materials.

b. Donated items become the property of SCLSNJ and may be added to the collection based upon the criteria for selection and retention established in the Collection Management Plan. Items not found to be suitable for the collection will be turned over to one of the SCLSNJ Friends of the Library groups for their use, marketed for sale for the benefit of SCLSNJ, or otherwise disposed of.

c. Because of changing needs and interests, relevancy, wear, theft, or damage of an item, SCLSNJ cannot guarantee the permanence of a gift placed in the collection.

d. Donors of money to purchase materials may specify the library branch that shall be the recipient of the gift. Donors may also specify to which subject area their gift shall apply.

e. While SCLSNJ will provide written acknowledgement of all donations, the Library does not appraise books and materials, and no dollar value will be assigned to any donated items.

Approved 02/3/10
Amended 12/7/16
Amended 4/5/17

FIGURE 5.4
(continued)

Auburn Public Library

The policy at Auburn Public Library has a good foundation by starting off with a purpose statement. It is one of the few policies that provides guidance to both employees and patrons about Section 107 Fair Use. See figure 5.5.

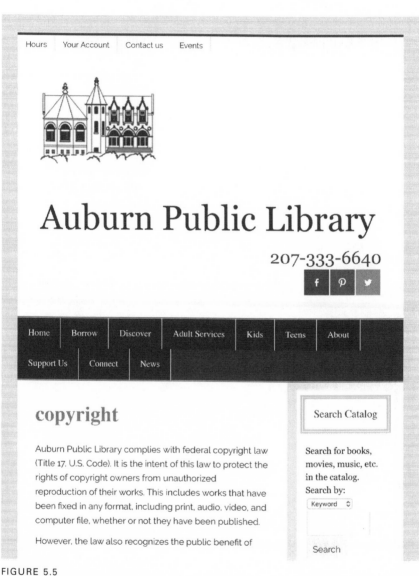

FIGURE 5.5

Copyright Policy. *Auburn Public Library, http://www.auburnpubliclibrary.org/about-the -library/apl-policies/copyright/.*

allowing citizens to do limited copying from copyrighted works for educational purposes. Under the precepts of **fair use** (section 107), library patrons may copy or print parts of copyrighted works for one-time, educational, non-profit activities. Copying that would replace or infringe upon a commercial sale of a copyrighted work (such as copying a work in its entirety, copying something for repeated use, or making exceedingly numerous copies of the same item) is forbidden. In such cases, library patrons should seek permission from the copyright owner before proceeding.

Public use of copy machines and printers

The library provides coin-operated photocopy machines and networked printers for the convenience and lawful use of its patrons. While library staff act in good faith by posting public notices and other practices to remind library patrons about copyright law and its restrictions, they cannot be liable for the acts of individual patrons using library materials or equipment.

Except in the case of filling interlibrary loan requests, library staff generally do not photocopy materials for patrons, although exceptions may be made when circumstances warrant.

Beyond those stipulated by the law, the Library places no restrictions on the photocopying of library materials by patrons, except in cases where fragile materials may be damaged during the photocopying process.

Staff practices

In the course of their work, library staff seek to adhere to the tenets of Title 17 and will not knowingly fulfill patron requests that constitute violations of copyright law.

For detailed guidelines about federal copyright law and how it pertains to library use and practices, see the American Library Association fact sheet on "Video and

Search this site

Search

Auburn Public Library

49 Spring St.
Auburn, ME 04210
207-333-6640
Hours
Summer hours are in effect between Memorial Day and Labor Day
Monday 9-8
Tuesday 9-6
Wednesday 9-6
Thursday 9-6
Friday 9-6
Saturday 9-1

Contact us

Lewiston Public Library
Auburn Public Schools

FIGURE 5.5
(continued)

King County Law Library

King County Law Library's policy begins with a purpose statement and sticks primarily to Section 108 Libraries & Archives. See figure 5.6.

COPYRIGHT POLICY & INTELLECTUAL PROPERTY STATEMENT

The King County Law Library will place a notice of copyright ownership on its original works of authorship, including works created by Law Library employees within the scope of their employment. The notice will include a statement that grants permission for copying of these materials by other parties for educational purposes without prior permission from the Law Library. Authorship must be attributed to the King County Law Library.

Unsupervised Copying By Patrons:

A. Copying Equipment

Copying equipment is made available to patrons for their copying needs. The Law Library has prominently posted on all copying equipment the following notice:

Copyright Notice

The copyright law of the United States (title17, United States Code) governs the making of photocopies or other reproductions of copyrighted material.

The person using this equipment is liable for any infringement.

B. Computer Disks

When a publisher provides a computer disk, the disk may be signed out. The Law Library will attach copyright labels to all computer disk packages to notify users that the United States copyright laws govern any reproduction of the disk contents. The warning shall consist of the following language:

The copyright law of the United States (title 17, United States Code) governs the reproduction, distribution, adaptation, public performance, and public display of copyrighted material.

Under certain conditions specified in law, nonprofit libraries are authorized to lend, lease, or rent copies of computer

FIGURE 5.6

Copyright Policy & Intellectual Property Statement. *King County Law Library, http://kcll .org/contact-us/policies/copyright-policy-intellectual-property-statement/.*

programs to patrons on a nonprofit basis and for nonprofit purposes. Any person who makes an unauthorized copy or adaptation of the computer program, or redistributes the loan copy, or publicly performs or displays the computer program, except as permitted by title 17 of the United States Code, may be liable for copyright infringement.

This institution reserves the right to refuse to fulfill a loan request if, in its judgment, fulfillment of the request would lead to violation of the copyright law.

Document Delivery Services:

The Law Library collection is open to the public. As an enhanced service, subscribers may request a copy that the Law Library will provide at the costs incurred, without purpose of direct or indirect commercial advantage. Each copy will include a notice of copyright. An authorized representative for each account is required to sign a Copyright Compliance form that is kept on file with the Public Law Library. The language on the form consists of the following:

NOTICE WARNING CONCERNING COPYRIGHT RESTRICTIONS

The copyright law of the United States (title 17, United States Code) governs the making of photocopies or other reproductions of copyrighted material.

Under certain conditions specified in the law, libraries and archives are authorized to furnish a photocopy or other reproduction. One of these specific conditions is that the photocopy or reproduction is not to be "used for any purpose other than private study, scholarship, or research." If a user makes a request for, or later uses, a photocopy or reproduction for purposes in excess of "fair use," that user may be liable for copyright infringement.

This institution reserves the right to refuse to accept a copying order if, in its judgment, fulfillment of the order would involve violation of copyright law.

When a request is made, the Law Library staff will check to verify that such a form has been signed and filed with the Law Library. If the form is on file, the requestor will be reminded that they have signed the form. If they need to review this form, a copy will be faxed to them. If they do not have a form on file, one will be faxed to them. The Copyright Compliance form must be signed and faxed back to the Law Library before the request will be processed. Each subsequent time an order is placed, the staff member will remind the requestor of the form and their agreement to abide by it.

The Law Library will observe the following guidelines when responding to a request from a subscriber. No more than one article or contribution from an issue or collected work will be copied per request. Multiple copies of the same material for related subscribers will not be made and no title will be systematically reproduced for a subscriber. All copies will become the property of the subscriber and copies used for faxing purposes will be destroyed. Each document within an order will include the notice of copyright provided by the publisher or, when such notice can not be located in the publication, will be individually stamped with a notice of copyright. The Law Library reserves the right to deny a request to copy which, in its judgment, exceeds fair use as defined in title 17 United States Code § 107.

Preservation/Replacement Copying:

All Law Library copying for purposes of collection preservation or replacement of previously purchased materials will comply with the statutory requirements of 17 United States Code § 108, including a diligent search for a replacement at a fair price.

Adopted 03/17/1999
Revised 06/13/2011

FIGURE 5.6
(continued)

National Park Service Copyright Policy

The National Park Service's policy on the use of copyrighted works is unique among these sample documents because it incorporates public performance and display. Most copyright policies, as we have seen, focus on exceptions such as fair use, libraries & archives, and face-to-face teaching. This one emphasizes a requirement to obtain permission when NPS employees show a movie, play music, or display other kinds of copyrighted works. This policy would apply to National Park Services (NPS) librarians and information professionals. See figure 5.7.

Guidance on the Public Display or Performance of a Copyrighted Work

The following guidance on the public display or performance of a copyrighted work was prepared by the DOI Solicitor's Office. It is intended to help National Park Service staff understand the need to obtain permission from a copyright holder before publicly showing a film, film clip, playing music or performing or displaying other copyrighted works.

A note on the sample permission language (page 3): The sample wording assumes that a fee will be paid by the National Park Service, but a zero sum may be entered if the copyright holder allows free use. In many cases the copyright holder will have specific language it requires in a license agreement. If the copyright holder does not require specific language, use this sample language. Before signing any license agreement provided to you by a copyright holder, consult with your local or regional solicitor. The language in this sample is excerpted from the federal acquisition regulation, FAR 52.227-17 Rights in Data, Special Works.

9-28-2018

FIGURE 5.7
Guidance on the Public Display or Performance of a Copyrighted Work. *National Park Service, https://www.nps.gov/policy/Public_Display_or_Performance_of_Copyrighted_Work.pdf.*

Public Display or Performance of a Copyrighted Work

Federal copyright law provides the owner of a copyright the **EXCLUSIVE** right to publicly display or perform the copyrighted work. This includes the showing of a film or film clip. In other words, unless you are the copyright owner, or else have permission from the owner, a public display or performance of a film, film clip or other copyrighted work is considered infringement.

Infringement of a copyright can bring civil liability in the form of monetary damages and also, depending on the facts surrounding the infringement, can bring criminal fines and penalties.

The federal government does not enjoy any immunity or special treatment with regard to copyright infringement. We, as federal employees, will suffer the same consequences as anyone else who infringes a copyright. Likewise, not-for-profit copyright infringement is *still* copyright infringement. The nonprofit status of the infringer is irrelevant in determining whether a copyright infringement has occurred.

Allowing others to infringe a copyright within a park or for the benefit of a park is not permissible. The legal mechanisms of "contributory infringement" and "vicarious infringement" may be used to impose liability on the park in such a situation. Before issuing a site permit, or otherwise allowing a public display or performance of a copyrighted work, the park must exercise diligence in requiring and verifying that the appropriate permission from the copyright owner has been obtained. Additionally, the park should use indemnification provisions in the park use permits to further limit liability arising out of a copyright infringement in which the park is not directly involved.

No discussion about copyright infringement would be complete without some attention being paid to fair use. While it is true that there are certain defenses to copyright infringement, with the primary defense being fair use, relying on such a defense should occur only upon the advice of legal counsel. Legal advice is essential in such a situation because the necessary analysis is very fact specific and nuanced. It is absolutely imperative to understand that "fair use" is a defense to an infringement claim rather than a right or exception serving to circumvent a lawsuit. In other words, a favorable fair use analysis does not preclude an infringement claim but rather, assesses the likelihood of a successful defense to the claim. Many people incorrectly believe that educational and/or nonprofit use broadly provides an exception to copyright infringement. However, these circumstances are not infringement exceptions but rather, are considerations applicable to a fair use analysis and possibly, a fair use defense.

Relying on a fair use defense as a means to infringe a copyright always involves some sort of risk. For this reason, fair use should be used only as a last resort and never used to circumvent a readily available, reasonably priced license. With regard to popular films, licenses for most films may be obtained from one of the following:

Criterion Pictures
www.criterionpicusa.com
(800) 890-9494

Motion Picture Licensing Corporation
www.mplc.org
(800) 462-8855

Swank Motion Pictures, Inc.
www.swank.com
(800) 876-5577

9-28-2018

FIGURE 5.7
(continued)

Sample Language for Copyright Owner to Grant Permission to NPS

INSERT GRANTEE NAME grants to the Government, and others acting on its behalf, a paid-up, nonexclusive, irrevocable, worldwide license for INSERT NAME OF WORK to (check as appropriate)

___reproduce

___prepare derivative works

___distribute copies to the public

___perform publicly and display publicly

by or on behalf of the Government.

A fee of _____ has been given to INSERT GRANTEE NAME to secure this permission to use INSERT NAME OF WORK.

INSERT GRANTEE NAME shall indemnify the Government and its officers, agents, and employees acting for the Government against any liability, including costs and expenses, incurred as the result of the violation of trade secrets, copyrights, or right of privacy or publicity, arising out of the creation, delivery, publication, or use of INSERT NAME OF WORK; or any libelous or other unlawful matter contained in INSERT NAME OF WORK.

9-28-2018

FIGURE 5.7
(continued)

LIBRARY PART OF PRIVATE, NONPROFIT SOCIETIES

LifeDiscoveryEd Digital Library

The copyright policy for LifeDiscoveryEd Digital Library has the dual role of obtaining permission from content providers and granting permission to library users. The policy does not include a mission statement, but instead lists the partner societies involved in establishing the digital library, which then grants permission for reuse through a Creative Commons license. See figure 5.8.

Copyright and Terms of Use

Copyright Policy for LifeDiscoveryEd Digital Library and all partner society portals.

Original copyright holders retain their rights to copyrighted materials submitted to LifeDiscoveryEd Digital Library or the partner portal, EcoEd Digital Library, EconBotEd Digital Library, PlantEd Digital Library or EvoEd Digital Library. Each partner professional Society - BSA, ESA, SEB and SSE - agree to give copyright holders appropriate credit in all reproductions, copies, and publications of the materials by the professional society.

Individuals submitting materials created or licensed by someone else must first obtain the original copyright holder's permission before sharing that resource via LifeDiscoveryEd Digital Library and all partner portals. Note that in some cases, the copyright holder for a resource may be a journal or publication, rather than an individual author. If this is the case, submitters must obtain permission from that publication as the licensor of the work. By granting their permission, copyright holders give the professional society the nonexclusive world rights to reproduce and/or distribute materials included in LifeDiscoveryEd Digital Library and all partner portals; this allows copyright holders to retain the rights to materials so that they may republish or otherwise use them.

Submitters of non-original work may use the Letter to Copyright Holders to obtain permission from original copyright holders. A signed copy of this letter must be sent to ESA, either to EcoEdDL@esa.org or to the following address:

Ecological Society of America
Office of Education and Diversity Programs
Attn: Jessica Johnston
1990 M St. NW
Suite 700
Washington, DC 20036

All users and submitters will be asked to agree to the LifeDiscoveryEd Digital Library copyright policy and terms of use when creating an account with LifeDiscoveryEd Digital Library or through any of the partner society portals.

Terms of Use

Copyrighted materials are licensed by the Ecological Society of America, Botanical Society of America, Society for the Study of Evolution and Society for Economic Botany under a Creative Commons Attribution-NonCommercial-ShareAlike 4.0 Unported License, represented by the symbol above. **Under this license, registered users of LifeDiscoveryDL are free to use, copy, distribute, and adapt resources under the following conditions:**

1. **All resources must be attributed to the original copyright holder,** but not in any way that suggests that the copyright holder endorses the user or their use of the resource.
2. **No resource shall be used for any commercial purpose.**
3. **Any alteration, transformation, or derivation of a resource may only be distributed using the same terms as this license.**

Exceptions:
The above conditions may be waived if permission is obtained from the copyright holder.
The above conditions do not apply to any works that are part of the public domain.

We strongly suggest that users read through the full provisions of the license before uploading any submissions to **LifeDiscoveryEd Digital Library or any of the partner portals** to ensure that all conditions are met. Email any questions to EcoEdDL@esa.org.

FIGURE 5.8

Copyright and Terms of Use. *Ecological Society of America, https://ecoed.esa.org/ Copyright.*

In this chapter, we explored sample copyright policies from eight different libraries. Each policy included a brief introductory paragraph highlighting the type of policy each document represented and the salient copyright components each policy included. The sample policies can assist librarians and information professionals who seek to establish or revise a copyright policy for their library.

Resources and Further Reading

This book covered the elements of creating a library copyright policy. We reviewed copyright basics, permissions, how to place your library in context, possible steps to take in drafting and implementing a policy, and sample workflows for using the policy in daily library operations.

For additional guidance and information, consult the following websites and books:

Websites about Copyright

ALA Copyright Tools. http://www.ala.org/advocacy/copyright-tools.

Code of Best Practices in Fair Use for Academic and Research Libraries. http://www.arl.org.

Copyright Clearance Center. http://copyright.com.

U.S. Copyright Office. https://www.copyright.gov.

U.S. Copyright Office Online Catalog of Registration Records. http://cocatalog .loc.gov.

Books about Copyright

The Copyright Book: A Practical Guide by William S. Strong.

Getting Permission: How to License & Clear Copyrighted Materials Online & Off by Richard Stim.

The Librarian's Copyright Companion, 2nd edition by James S. Heller, Paul Hellyer, and Benjamin J. Keele.

The Public Domain: How to Find & Use Copyright-Free Writings, Music, Art & More by Attorney Stephen Fishman.

Websites about Policy Writing

DIY Committee Guide. https://www.diycommitteeguide.org.

ePolicy Institute. http://www.epolicyinstitute.com.

National Conference of State Legislatures. http://www.ncsl.org/documents/legismgt/personnel_manual.pdf.

Policy Writing Tips. https://www.mtu.edu/policy/tips/.

Project Include. https://projectinclude.org.

Books about Policy Writing

The Government Manager's Guide to Plain Language by Judith G. Myers.

Practical Playscript: Writing Procedure Manuals That People Can Use by Robert Barnett.

Writing Effective Policies and Procedures: A Step-by-Step Resource for Clear Communication by Nancy Campbell.

Writing Public Policy: A Practical Guide to Communicating in the Policy Making Process by Catherine F. Smith.

Websites about Workflows

Efficient Librarian. https://efficientlibrarian.com.

Library Procedures: A Guide to Sanity. https://elementarylibrarian.com/library-procedures-guide-sanity/.

Library Publishing Workflows. https://librarypublishing.org/category/blog/workflows/.

Library Workflow Exchange. http://www.libraryworkflowexchange.org.

Tribal Library Procedures Manual. http://www.ala.org/aboutala/offices/olos/toolkits/trails.

Books about Workflows

Library Workflow Redesign: Six Case Studies by Marilyn Mitchell.

Management by Design: Applying Design Principles to the Work Experience by Daniel W. Rasmus.

The New Librarianship Field Guide by R. David Lankes.

Successful Business Process Management: What You Need to Know to Get Results by Paula K. Berman.

Index

About the Author

Allyson Mower, MA, MLIS is Associate Librarian and Head of Scholarly Communication & Copyright at the University of Utah Marriott Library. She has worked as a copyright librarian for more than ten years. Allyson provides the academic community and the general public with information, tools, and services related to both copyright and publishing. As a tenured faculty member, she researches the history of authorship and scholarly communication at the institution and writes about intellectual freedom and privacy for the American Library Association Intellectual Freedom Blog.

Currently, Allyson chairs the Copyright Education Committee of the Utah Library Association and provides workshops and training programs on copyright to Utah librarians. She has presented on copyright at various conferences including the Brigham Young University Copyright Symposium; Innovative Librarians Explore, Apply, and Discover (ILEAD); and the San Jose State University Open Access & Digital Repository Symposium.

Allyson was a *Library Journal* Mover & Shaker in 2008, was nominated as a 2012 Society for Scholarly Publishing Emerging Leader, and served as the Academic Senate President at the University of Utah in 2014.